Waffle It!

Waffle It!

101 Delicious Dishes to Create with Your Waffle Maker, Sandwich Maker, and Panini Press

Kate Woodson

© 2023 by Kate Woodson and Fox Chapel Publishing Company, Inc., 903 Square Street, Mount Joy, PA 17552.

Recipe selection, design, and book design © Fox Chapel Publishing. Recipes and photographs © G&R Publishing DBA CQ Products.

Shutterstock images: New Africa (back cover, top right); Kosoff (back cover, bottom left); solarus (back cover, top half illustration, verso folio illustration throughout); mihmihmal (back cover, bottom half illustration); Shawn Hempel (1, 3); MaxVasylenko (3, illustration) Rvector (waffle iron icon, throughout); linea vectors (sandwich maker icon, throughout); Brent Hofacker (9); Yuriy Golub (10, middle left); Zapylaiev Kostiantyn (10, top right, 13, bottom right); Commercial RAF (11); H_Ko (12).

ISBN 978-1-4971-0391-7

Library of Congress Control Number 2023940676

To learn more about the other great books from Fox Chapel Publishing, or to find a retailer near you, call toll-free 800-457-9112 or visit us at www.FoxChapelPublishing.com.

We are always looking for talented authors.
To submit an idea, please send a brief inquiry to
acquisitions@foxchapelpublishing.com.

Printed in China
First printing

Table of Contents

Introduction 9

What Is a Waffle? 10

Your Waffle Iron 11

Greasing Your Waffle Iron   12

Cleaning Your Waffle Iron   14

Additional Advice   15

Breakfast 16

Wheat Ale Waffles   18

Cinnamon-Apple Waffles   19

Golden Waffle Frittata   20

Quick Cinnamon Rolls   21

French Toast of the Town   21

Mini Muffin Crisps   22

Easy Cherry Turnovers   22

Cinnamon Peach French Toast   23

Banana Bites   24

Waffle-ly Good French Toast   26

The Breakfast Club   28

Toasted Bagel Sandwich   29

Donut Breakfast Sandwich   30

The Farmhand   30

Sweet Cinnamon Sandwich   31

The Lox Bagel   31

Lunch and Snacks 32

Spinach Wontons   34

Bacon & Avocado Bites   35

Tater Tot Flats   36

Reuben Waffles   38

18

22

28

39

45

56

Grilled Cheese Waffle	39
Chicken & Steak Fries	40
Greek Sliders	41
Barbecue Chicken Sandwich	42
Toasted BLT	43
Cheese & Onion Puffs	44
Inside-Out Jalapeño Poppers	45
Cobb Sandwich	46
Ultimate Greek Sandwich	46
Classic Italian	47
Spicy Sausage Sandwich	47
Cheesy Spinach Calzone	48
Stuffed Portobello Bake	49
Spinach Artichoke Sandwich	50
Pesto Panini	50
The Peachy Keen Sandwich	51
Fresh from the Garden Sandwich	51
Nacho Grilled Cheese	52
Apple Gruyère Sandwich	52
Parmesan Crisps	53
Field of Greens Sandwich	54
Prosciutto and Brie Sandwich	54
Broccoli Cheddar Sandwich	55
Pear and Bacon Sandwich	55
Beer-Battered Shrimp	56
The Sizzling Jalapeño Crunch	57
Brussels Sprout Melt	58
Turkey Pesto Sandwich	59
Five-Cheese Melt	59
Cheese-Studded Waffles	60

Waffle-Style Corn Dogs   62

Faux Fry Hodge Podge   64

Dinner 66

Pizza Waffles   68

Hawaiian Waffle Quesadillas   70

Monte Cristo   72

Leftover Spaghetti Melt   74

The Cordon Bleu   74

Barbecue Chicken Melt   75

Roast Beef Sandwich   75

Lasagna Waffles   76

Toasted Caprese Sandwich   78

Sassy Shrimp Sammy   78

Gouda Mushroom Melt   79

Toasted Turkey Sandwich   79

Eggplant Parm   80

The Frenchman   82

The Oktober-Feast   82

French Onion Steak Sandwich   83

Guacamole Galore   83

Waffled Crabby Patties   84

Stromboli Sandwich   86

Classic Reuben   86

Mac and Cheese Sammy   87

The Buffalo Ranch   87

Thanksgiving Leftovers   88

Chicken & Waffles Sandwich   90

Chipotle Mushroom Melt   90

Dill Corned Beef Sandwich   91

68

76

88

98

110

116

Chicken Parm Melt	91
Garden Veggie Calzones	92
Strawberry Turkey Panini	94
Luau Melt	95
Chipotle-Lime Roast Beef Sandwich	96
The Hot Potato	96
Fajita Sandwich	97
Cuban Sandwich	97
Buffalo Chicken Waffle	98
Waffle Cheeseburgers	100

The Sauces **102**

Chipotle Mayo	103
Creamy Honey Mustard	103
Chimichurri Sauce	103
Sriracha Soy Ketchup	103

Dessert **104**

Apple Tart	106
Strawberry Shorts	108
Waffle S'mores	110
Dessert Chimichangas	112
Glazed Donut Dippers	114
Ice Cream Waffle Sandwiches	116
Lemon Cake Stackers	118
Apple Pie Sandwich	120
Strawberry Cheesecake Sandwich	121
Sweet Banana Bread Sandwich	122
Toasted Pound Cake	123
Carrot Cake	124
Caramel Apple Delight	125

Index.. **126**

Introduction

Mmm, the waffle. Crispy on the outside, chewy on the inside, sweet, savory, lathered in syrup, or topped with fried chicken. The waffle is a classic American breakfast food, but it can be so much more. Waffles have a long history that started far outside the borders of American soil, dating all the way back to fourteenth-century France. The first waffle recipes even contained wine and cheese. In the fifteenth-century, the waffle recipe began to evolve and stretch to the lands of present-day Belgium, where waffle irons were beginning to look like the ones we know today. Then in the sixteenth century, a Belgian cookbook was published with the first waffle recipe to contain leavening. By this time, waffles had grown in popularity throughout Europe. Variations of the waffle recipe had come about in plenty of countries, with some more breadlike and others on the sweeter side.

The English language first heard the word "waffle" in the eighteenth century in a cookbook named *Court Cookery*. From there, the waffle spread to America where it was adopted as a beloved piece of European cuisine. And although Americans established their own versions of the waffle recipe, many of those recipes can be traced to Dutch, French, Belgian, or German origins. However the original waffle makers envisioned their waffles to be, they never could have imagined how substantial their creation would be to future generations.

Today, waffles are served sweet or savory and topped with syrup, whipped cream, fried chicken, fruit, and many other classic favorites. However, this book introduces a variety of fun, unique recipes to spice up your waffle-making game! From strawberry shortcakes, sweet apple tarts, and banana bites to cheesy waffle tots, veggie calzones, lasagna, and pizza

Waffles are delicious as a classic breakfast food, but the possibilities of waffle-making are almost endless!

pockets, you'll devour waffles like never before! Now you don't have to bust out the waffle iron just for breakfast; you can use it for all meals of the day. And if you're pressed for time, waffle iron recipes are easy to prep, ready in minutes, and require minimal cleanup!

Something else this book does is pose the question: What is a waffle? You know the history and common characteristics, but I'll also dive deeper into the brass tacks of waffling: a hot iron pressing down on ingredients to present a crispy, melt-in-your-mouth meal. Yes, it's really that simple. So, whether you're making food for your whole family or flying solo, the recipes in this book are sure to crush your hunger and curb your cravings. Let's waffle!

What Is a Waffle?

According to Merriam-Webster's dictionary, a waffle is "a crisp cake of batter baked in a waffle iron." Well, in this book, I'll show you that a waffle can be made up of a lot more than just batter. And you can use a waffle iron if you'd like, or you can use a handy tool called the sandwich maker (or panini press). So, for the purposes of this book, if you put batter, dough, bread, or even a donut in between two hot irons and toast it until it's crunchy, that's a waffle in my book. And that's also part of what makes waffling so fun! You aren't constrained to the traditional waffle-iron-and-batter combo—although I have plenty of those recipes for you to try. Each recipe in this book will have an icon (either a waffle iron or a sandwich maker) to suggest the best hot iron to waffle with—but feel free to switch it up! The moral of the story, no matter what iron you use, is: have fun, take risks, and waffle it!

A sandwich maker or panini press allows you to press together your ingredients until you're left with a crunchy, melty, delicious meal—just like a waffle maker!

Look For One Of These Icons!

Waffle Maker

Sandwich Maker

The classic waffle maker, as shown here, creates a traditional-looking waffle. Once the light is green, it's ready to cook your batter to crispy perfection.

Your Waffle Iron

If you already own a waffle iron, then it's likely you've gotten to know it already. But if you're in the market for one, it's important to know that all waffle irons are different, but they all do the same thing: make delicious waffles! They can be round, square, big, small, have different features, and be made with different nonstick coating. There are classic irons, Belgian irons, flipping irons, ceramic irons, mini irons, removable-plate irons, four-slice irons, bowl irons, character irons, double-flip irons, stovetop irons, and more! No matter what you choose, you'll get the same result.

Do some research before buying to make sure you're getting the iron that will be the best fit for you! For these recipes, a bigger

Although the mini waffle iron, here, is cute, it may not be able to handle more hearty recipes. Use this for a smaller snack waffle.

surface area is recommended. The mini waffle iron is convenient and cute but won't be the best option for these hearty recipes. *Consider that most of these recipes are tested on a four-slice waffle iron, while some are tested on a classic iron.*

Waffle irons can be a bit tricky when determining how much batter to use. It's important to note that most of these recipes don't involve traditional batter and include other components that can potentially overwhelm the iron's surface. Keep this in mind when piling ingredients onto your iron. As you can tell, a lot of the waffle-making process relies on personal preference, like

This four-slice waffle iron creates four square waffles at once: perfect for serving the whole family in a short amount of time!

Making a delicious waffle starts with the right waffle iron.

Before you begin toasting, make sure all your ingredients are prepared and ready for the waffling.

Greasing Your Waffle Iron

Nonstick waffle irons are a great starting point for ensuring your waffles don't stick. Much of the market has Teflon™-coated nonstick surfaces while others are ceramic. If you have a Teflon nonstick waffle maker, greasing can sometimes do more harm than good. As much as I love using cooking spray for its convenience, this can ruin your nonstick surface over time and make it harder to clean. So, please, avoid the cooking spray! If you love adding butter to your nonstick surface for buttery flavor, do so sparingly and apply only with a silicon brush. However, butter can also cause damage to your Teflon-coated iron surface if you're not careful, and can also cause extra cleanup. The same rules apply for ceramic nonstick irons, but you're free to

The classic waffle iron molds its batter to a square, grid-like pattern, and a similar effect can be accomplished with a sandwich maker. Most irons have built-in textures that add not only crunch, but pizzazz to your meal.

adjusting the heat. Note that some recipes will list a specific temperature, but the rest are up to you. And no need to set a timer! Like a toaster, your waffle iron will automatically set a time depending on the heat setting and will indicate when it is finished by beeping or signaling with a light. If it's not browned enough, you can go another round at a lower heat setting until it's done to your liking. Just keep an eye on it!

And finally, if you're feeling adventurous—and you have one on hand—try a panini press! There are multiple sandwich recipes included in this book that would be equally tasty if made panini-style. The waffle iron and panini press are like cousins; don't be afraid to explore what they can do! The possibilities are endless.

Be sure to properly grease your waffle iron so the finished waffle comes off the iron with ease.

use butter or oil if you want the extra flavor (Always apply with a silicon brush!). However, it's not necessary. You can always add the butter after your waffles are finished! Now, if you have a classic cast-iron waffle maker, you do need to grease it if it's not seasoned. You can use oil or butter to do so. But if your cast iron is well-seasoned, don't worry about greasing! It should work just as well as any other nonstick waffle iron. If you own none of the above, this means you own a non-nonstick iron! In that case, grease with butter or oil, still using a silicon brush to avoid scratching the surface.

Note: If the recipe calls for greasing your iron, feel free to do so with the above intel in mind.

But what if your waffles start to stick? Many waffle makers run into this problem, but it doesn't always mean you need to grease them.

Turning the heat up can help fix the sticking dilemma. If your waffle iron isn't producing enough heat, the inside of your waffle will remain raw, causing the outsides to stick to the hot surface and fall apart. To prevent any mishaps, make sure your waffle iron is fully preheated before placing the batter on the iron. Also doing a deep clean of your iron can help stop the sticking (see Cleaning Your Waffle Iron). Thickening your waffle batter may improve the situation. If your batter is too thin, you can add more dry ingredients to thicken it. If none of these solve the sticking issue, perhaps your nonstick coating is wearing down (if your waffle iron is on the older side, or if you have used cooking spray in the past). If that is the case, greasing will be necessary to avoid sticking. Consider purchasing a new iron if your nonstick coating is no longer nonstick.

A removable-plate waffle iron, shown here, makes cleaning a breeze. Just pop out the stainless-steel bottom and clean away!

Cleaning Your Waffle Iron

Don't worry, your whole kitchen won't need a deep clean after making waffles, but your waffle iron might! Because some of these recipes are nontraditional recipes that require cheese, bread, vegetables, and meats, you should be prepared to clean up whatever ingredients ooze out the side of your waffle iron. To minimize the amount of spilling, start with less ingredients on your waffle iron to get an idea for how much it can take at once. Remember, all waffle irons are different! Get to know yours by testing out its limits to avoid a messy countertop. Tip: Put paper towels, newspaper, or washable hand towels under your waffle iron to catch any spills! If your iron has seen better days, the cleaning process may be more thorough. Sometimes a deep clean can also help prevent any sticking mishaps. If your iron is on the newer side, cleaning will be easier but is just as important.

When it comes time to clean up, always unplug your waffle iron and let it cool down before starting the process. Also, check the waffle iron manual for any cleanup techniques intended specifically for your iron. If you're missing a manual, that's alright! You can also search online for specific instructions for your model OR keep reading here for the most basic way to go about cleaning your iron.

Start by using a paper towel to remove any excess batter, butter, oil, or crumbs from the iron's surface. For any stubborn batter, use a rubber spatula to lift and remove it. If something

No need to worry about overfilling your iron with batter—cleanup is easy!

still isn't coming off, apply any kind of oil on hard clumps and let it sit for 10 minutes, then gently scrape them off with your rubber spatula.

Only complete this step if your iron still appears dirty, or your iron has grease residue on it: Apply baking soda to a soft brush or paper towel. Gently scrub the iron's surface, never applying too much pressure.

When your iron is finally free of any batter, grease, and other ingredients, use a damp cloth to thoroughly wipe the iron's surface. Make sure to wipe the outside, too.

Leave your waffle iron open to dry, making sure it is completely dry before putting it away.

Never scrub your waffle iron with harsh, abrasive tools! Don't submerge it in water or get the iron's surface fully wet unless otherwise directed by the waffle iron manual. Most cases will only require you to wipe the surface with a paper towel!

Additional Advice

- Always wait for the waffle maker to beep or for its light to turn on before opening it.
- Use a fork, spoon, butter knife, or chopsticks to get your waffle creation off the iron when it's done. Be careful not to scrape the surface or burn yourself!
- It's okay if your waffle doesn't look perfect the first time! This is a normal part of the waffle-making process.
- You can keep your oven on warm to house the cooked waffles while you finish the rest of the batter.
- Pre-prepping your ingredients saves even more time, but it's not necessary.
- Preheating your iron before gathering ingredients will save time. That way when you're ready to use the iron, it'll be ready for you!

Once you master the waffle iron, you can begin to have fun and figure out what kind of waffles you can make, like this pizza waffle.

Breakfast

◇◇◇◇◇◇◇◇◇◇◇◇◇◇◇◇◇◇◇◇◇◇◇◇◇◇◇◇◇◇◇◇◇◇◇◇◇

When you think of waffles, you probably automatically think of breakfast. The recipes in this section will give you that classic waffle feeling—sweet, fresh fruits, and smoky meats—while also introducing some new ideas to keep breakfast fun. Plus, check out the recipes that are perfect for the panini press for an extra jolt of warm, toasty deliciousness. Get ready to crunch, smile, and take another bite!

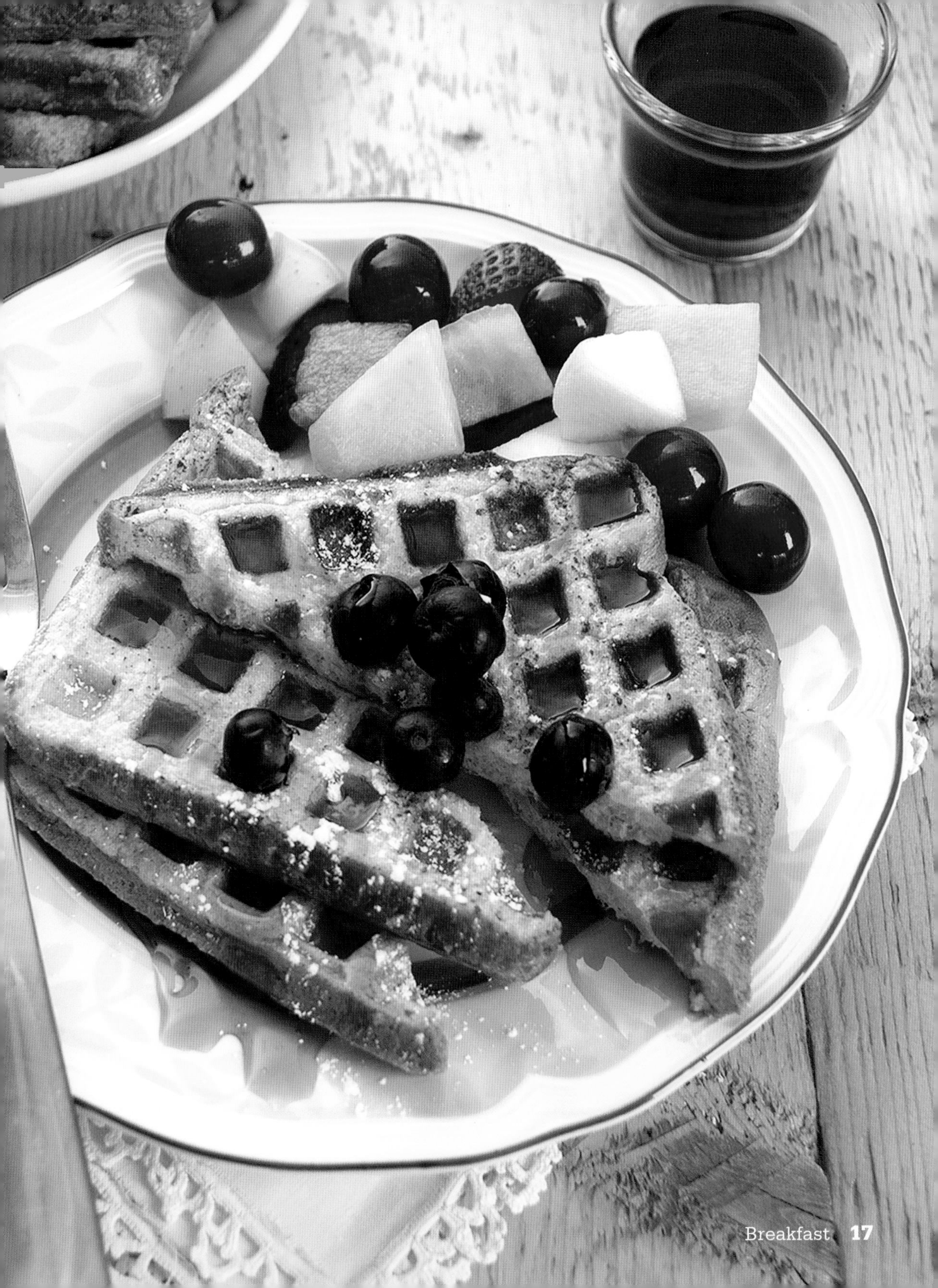

Wheat Ale Waffles

Ingredients

» 2 cups flour
» 1 teaspoon baking powder
» ½ teaspoon baking soda
» ¼ teaspoon salt
» 2 tablespoons sugar
» 2 large eggs, lightly beaten
» 1 cup wheat ale
» ¾ cup milk
» ¼ cup butter, melted
» ½ teaspoon vanilla extract
» 1 teaspoon orange zest, plus more for garnish
» Powdered sugar, whipped cream, and maple syrup, for topping

Serves 5

1. Preheat your waffle iron according to manufacturer directions.

2. In a large bowl, whisk together the flour, baking powder, baking soda, salt, and sugar; set aside.

3. In a separate bowl, combine the eggs, wheat ale, milk, butter, vanilla extract, and orange zest. Add the egg mixture to the flour mixture and fold together until just combined.

4. Cook the waffles according to manufacturer directions.

5. Serve warm, topped with powdered sugar, whipped cream, maple syrup, and orange zest. Enjoy!

Cinnamon-Apple Waffles

Ingredients

- » 1 ½ cups flour
- » ¾ teaspoon ground cinnamon
- » ½ teaspoon baking soda
- » ⅛ teaspoon baking powder
- » ½ teaspoon salt
- » 1 egg plus 1 egg white
- » 1 cup sugar
- » ½ cup vegetable oil
- » 1 ½ teaspoons vanilla
- » 1 cup peeled and finely chopped Golden Delicious apple
- » ¼ cup finely chopped walnuts

1. Preheat your waffle iron and coat it lightly with oil.

2. In a small bowl, mix the flour, cinnamon, baking soda, baking powder, and salt.

3. In a medium bowl, beat the egg and egg white; add the sugar and oil and beat until well blended. Stir in the vanilla and the flour mixture. The batter will be thick.

4. Toss the apple and walnuts in the mix and give it a good stir. Now you're ready to waffle it.

5. Pour some batter onto the hot iron, close the lid, and bake until done.

6. Drizzle with a little melted butter and this bread will simply melt in your mouth.

Golden Waffle Frittata

Serves 4

Ingredients

» 4 eggs
» 2 tablespoons half-and-half
» 6 fully cooked bacon strips, crumbled
» ½ cup shredded cheese (I used sharp cheddar)
» ¼ cup tomato, chopped
» 3 green onions, sliced
» Salt and pepper, to taste

1. Preheat and lightly grease your waffle iron.

2. In a bowl, whisk together the eggs and half-and-half until well blended. Stir in the bacon, cheese, tomato, green onions, salt, and pepper.

3. Pour part of the mixture onto the hot iron, close the lid, and cook until the eggs are done to your liking. Serve and enjoy!

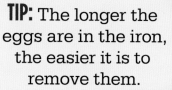

TIP: The longer the eggs are in the iron, the easier it is to remove them.

Quick Cinnamon Rolls

Serves 8

Ingredients
» 1 tube refrigerator cinnamon rolls
» Store-bought frosting, for topping

1. Preheat and grease the waffle iron.
2. Place a few individual rolls from the tube of cinnamon rolls on the hot iron; close and cook until golden brown and no longer doughy.
3. Repeat with the remaining rolls.
4. Spread frosting on top of the hot rolls and serve.

French Toast of the Town

Serves 1

Ingredients
» 1 egg plus 1 egg, scrambled
» ¼ cup milk
» 1 teaspoon vanilla
» ¼ teaspoon cinnamon
» ¼ teaspoon nutmeg
» 2 thick-cut Italian bread slices
» 2 frozen hashbrowns, cooked
» 2 slices Brie cheese
» 2 cooked bacon slices (crispy)
» Salt, to taste
» Maple syrup, for dipping

1. For the batter, combine 1 egg and the milk, vanilla, cinnamon, and nutmeg in a bowl.
2. Dip one side of a bread slice in the batter and place it in a greased panini press.
3. Layer the remaining ingredients and top with another dipped bread slice.
4. Toast both sides. Serve with maple syrup for dipping.

Mini Muffin Crisps

Servings Vary

Ingredients
» Blueberry muffin mix
» Softened butter, to taste

1. Preheat and grease your waffle iron.

2. Whip up a batch of blueberry muffins from a mix (or your favorite recipe).

3. Drop the batter by the tablespoon onto the waffle iron.

4. Close and cook until the muffins are done.

5. Spread softened butter over the top of the hot muffin crisps so you can enjoy all those little pools of melted goodness.

6. Serve and enjoy!

Easy Cherry Turnovers

Serves 6

Ingredients
» 1 package refrigerated fill-and-bake turnovers
» Frosting, for topping

1. Preheat and grease your waffle iron.

2. Assemble refrigerated fill-and-bake turnovers as directed on the package.

3. Set a couple of turnovers on the hot iron, close, and cook until golden brown and no longer doughy.

4. Repeat with the remaining turnovers. Drizzle with frosting when done. Enjoy!

Cinnamon Peach French Toast

Ingredients

Batter:
» 1 egg
» ¼ cup milk
» 1 teaspoon vanilla
» ¼ teaspoon cinnamon
» ¼ teaspoon sugar

Toast:
» 2 cinnamon swirl bread slices
» 1 ounce cream cheese
» 1 ounce pecans, chopped
» 4 fresh peach slices
» Maple syrup, for serving

Serves 1

1. Whisk together the ingredients for the batter.

2. Dip one side of one bread slice into the egg mixture and set it into a greased iron, egg side down.

3. Add the cream cheese, pecans, and peaches. Top with another dipped bread slice, egg side up.

4. Close the iron and toast to perfection. Serve with maple syrup and enjoy!

Banana Bites

1. Stir together the flour, cornstarch, coconut, sugar, baking powder, and salt. Add the egg yolks, milk, and vanilla. Mash one banana and stir it into the mixture.

2. Preheat and lightly grease your waffle iron.

3. Peel one banana. Slice it in half crosswise and then slice each half lengthwise (you'll have four banana pieces). Dunk each piece into the batter and remove the excess batter.

4. Place the pieces on the hot iron, close the lid, and cook until toasty brown and the edges are cooked. Repeat with the remaining bananas.

5. Serve with syrup and/ or honey on the side if you'd like.

NOW TRY THIS

If you have batter remaining, just place small mounds of it in the waffle iron and cook until done. They'll still taste great—and have a hint of banana flavor.

Ingredients

- » ½ cup flour
- » ½ cup cornstarch
- » ⅓ cup sweetened flaked (or toasted) coconut
- » 2 tablespoons sugar
- » ½ teaspoon baking powder
- » Pinch of salt
- » 2 egg yolks
- » ¼ cup plus 1 tablespoon milk
- » ¼ teaspoon vanilla
- » 7 firm bananas, divided

Waffle-ly Good French Toast

Serves 3

1. Preheat and lightly grease your waffle iron.
2. Whisk together the eggs, milk, vanilla, sugar, and cinnamon until very well blended.
3. One at a time, dip bread slices in the egg mixture and place them on the iron. Close the lid and bake until golden brown.
4. Serve this French toast your favorite way.

Ingredients
- » 2 eggs
- » ⅓ cup milk
- » ½ teaspoon vanilla
- » 1 ½ teaspoons sugar
- » ¼ teaspoon cinnamon
- » 6 bread slices

WHY WAFFLE IT?

No more soggy French toast. The waffle iron takes care of that wiggly, too-soft middle, leaving you with the nice texture of this toast. Try using French bread, cinnamon-swirl bread, or any other bread you enjoy for extra flavor.

The Breakfast Club

Ingredients
» Butter, as needed
» 2 multigrain bread slices
» 1 tablespoon raspberry jam
» 2 slices Provolone cheese
» 2 thin slices prosciutto
» 2 slices deli roast turkey breast
» 1 egg, cooked over easy
» Fresh arugula, to taste
» Black pepper, to taste

Serves 1

1. Butter one side of each slice of bread.

2. Spread jam on the unbuttered side of the bread.

3. Layer the remaining ingredients between the slices and toast in a panini press. Serve warm and enjoy!

Toasted Bagel Sandwich

Ingredients

» 2 Bagel Thins
» 2 precooked eggs
» Salt and pepper, to taste
» 1 slice American cheese
» 1 slice Canadian bacon

1. Set the bagel halves inside a greased iron.

2. Place the eggs on one side and sprinkle with salt and pepper.

3. Layer on the cheese and Canadian bacon. (Keep the cheese in the middle so it doesn't melt through the hole in the bagel.)

4. Close the iron and toast until the bagel has browned up nicely. The cheese will be hot and melty. Enjoy!

Donut Breakfast Sandwich

Serves 1

Ingredients

- » Butter, as needed
- » 1 maple-frosted donut, sliced in half
- » 2 slices cooked bacon (crispy)
- » 2 slices Muenster cheese

1. Butter one side of each slice of donut.
2. Layer all the other ingredients between the donut halves and toast in a panini press. Enjoy!

1. Butter one side of each slice of bread or muffin.
2. Layer the remaining ingredients between the bread slices and toast in a panini press. Serve and enjoy!

The Farmhand

Serves 1

Ingredients

- » Butter, as needed
- » 1 English muffin, split, or 2 white bread slices
- » 1 egg, cooked over easy
- » 4 leaves fresh baby spinach
- » 1 slice sharp cheddar cheese
- » 2 slices cooked bacon (crispy)

Sweet Cinnamon Sandwich

Serves 1

1. Butter one side of each slice of bread.

2. Spread mascarpone on the unbuttered side of the bread.

3. Layer all the remaining ingredients between the bread slices and toast both sides in a panini press. Enjoy!

Ingredients
» Butter, as needed
» 2 cinnamon raisin bread slices
» 2 tablespoons mascarpone
» ½ cup blueberries
» ½ cup semisweet chocolate chips

The Lox Bagel

Serves 1

Ingredients
» Butter, as needed
» 1 everything bagel, sliced
» 1 tablespoon cream cheese, softened
» 1 slice Gruyère cheese
» 2 ounces Nova lox
» 2 slices red onion
» 1 teaspoon capers
» Fresh dill, to taste

1. Butter one side of each slice of bagel.

2. Spread the cream cheese on the unbuttered side of the bagel.

3. Layer the remaining ingredients between the bagel halves and toast both sides in a panini press. Enjoy!

Lunch and Snacks

Waffles don't have to be eaten strictly for hearty meals. These recipes prove that you can put delicious ingredients in your waffle maker for a quick, anytime snack or light lunch. From light bites to toasty sandwiches, these lunch recipes will have you wanting to waffle all your foodl!

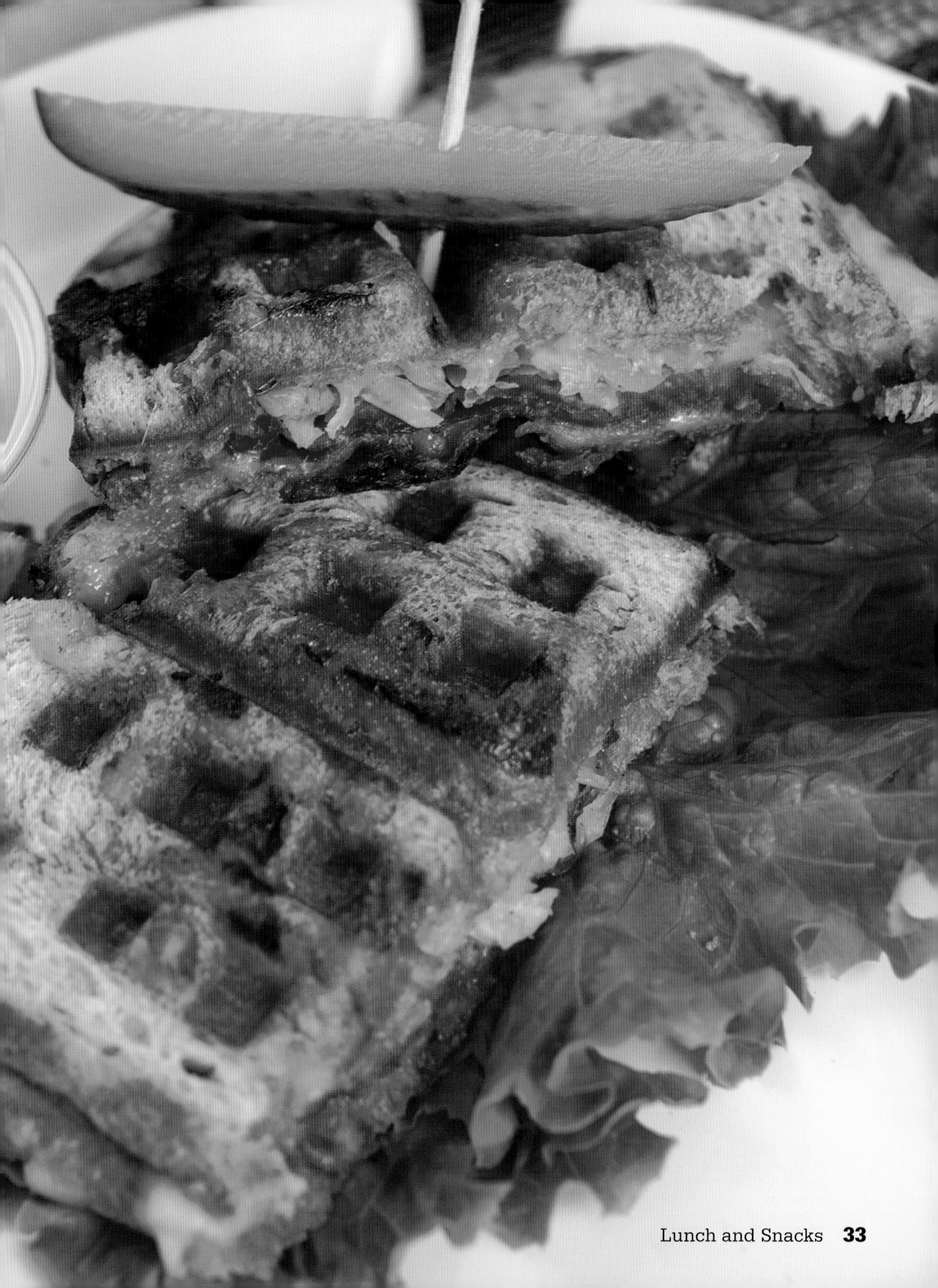

Spinach Wontons

Ingredients

» 1 (8 ounce) package cream cheese, softened

» 1 (10 ounce) package frozen spinach, thawed and squeezed dry

» ½ teaspoon garlic salt

» ½ teaspoon coarse black pepper

» Pinch of cayenne pepper

» 24 wonton wrappers

 **Serves 24**

1. Preheat and grease your waffle iron.

2. Stir together the cream cheese, spinach, garlic salt, black pepper, and cayenne pepper together in a mixing bowl.

3. Place 2 to 3 teaspoons of the spinach mixture on each of the wonton wrappers; wet the edges of the wrappers with water and fold in half, pressing the edges to seal.

4. Set the wontons on the hot iron; close and cook until nicely browned. Enjoy immediately.

Bacon & Avocado Bites

 **Serves 1**

Ingredients

» Butter, as needed
» 2 (¼-inch-thick) ciabatta bread slices
» Avocado, thinly sliced, to taste
» Bacon, cooked, to taste
» Shredded Colby cheese, to taste

1. Preheat your waffle iron.

2. For each serving, butter one side of the bread slices.

3. On the unbuttered side, stack thin slices of avocado and cooked bacon; sprinkle with shredded Colby cheese.

4. Place the other bread slice on top, buttered side out. Place on the hot waffle iron, close, and cook until perfectly toasted. Enjoy!

Tater Tot Flats

Serves 2

1. Preheat and lightly grease your waffle iron (if your iron has a browning control setting, set it on high).

2. Coat the tater tots with cooking spray.

3. Stir together the parsley flakes, seasoned salt, dry mustard, and pepper; sprinkle evenly over the tots.

4. Arrange the tots close together in the iron. Set the lid down gently and bake until deep brown and crispy, pressing down lightly on the handle occasionally so the tots in the front get done (use a hot pad).

5. Serve with ketchup for dipping and enjoy!

Ingredients

» 1 package onion-flavored tater tots, thawed
» ¼ teaspoon dried parsley flakes
» ¼ teaspoon seasoned salt
» ¼ teaspoon dry mustard
» ¼ teaspoon pepper
» Ketchup, for dipping

WHY WAFFLE IT?

You get all the crunch, all the way through. And the seasoning mix just makes them even more scrumptious!

How do you like your tater tots? If you like them hot, brown, and crispy,
you've come to the right place. Behold the power of the waffle iron.

Reuben Waffles

Serves 1

Ingredients

» 2 rye bread slices
» Thousand island dressing, to taste
» Swiss cheese, thinly sliced, to taste
» Pastrami or corned beef, thinly sliced, to taste
» Sauerkraut, drained and squeezed to remove excess moisture, to taste
» Butter, as needed
» Lettuce, for garnish
» Pickle, for garnish

1. Preheat your waffle iron.

2. Spread one side of the bread with thousand island dressing.

3. To the coated side of one slice, add thin layers of Swiss cheese, pastrami or corned beef, and sauerkraut.

4. Put the other bread slice on top, coated side in.

5. Butter the outsides, set the sandwich on the hot waffle iron, close, and cook until golden brown. Garnish with lettuce and a pickle. Enjoy!

Grilled Cheese Waffle

Serves 1

Ingredients

» Butter, as needed
» 2 multigrain bread slices
» American cheese slices, to taste
» Swiss cheese slices, to taste
» Gouda cheese, sliced to taste

1. Preheat your waffle iron.
2. Butter one side of each bread slice.
3. On the unbuttered side, layer cheeses heartily.
4. Place the remaining bread slice on top, buttered side out.
5. Set on the hot waffle iron, close, and cook until toasty.
6. Serve and enjoy the cheesy goodness.

Chicken & Steak Fries

Servings Vary

Ingredients

- » Frozen chicken strips, as needed
- » Frozen seasoned steak fries, as needed
- » Ketchup, ranch, or other dip, for dipping

1. Thaw frozen chicken strips and seasoned steak fries.

2. Preheat your waffle iron.

3. Pop them onto the hot waffle iron, close, and cook until heated through. (You can cook them together if your chicken strips and fries are uniform in thickness; otherwise, it's best to cook them separately.)

4. Serve with ketchup, ranch, or any other dip you prefer.

Greek Sliders

Serves 1

Ingredients

» 1 slice sourdough bread
» 2 tablespoons hummus
» 2 cucumber slices
» 2 slices deli roast turkey
» 2 slices red pepper, roasted
» 2 slices Provolone cheese
» Butter, as needed

1. Spread the hummus onto the sourdough bread; cut the bread into quarters.

2. Top two of the quarters with one cucumber slice, deli sliced roast turkey, roasted red pepper, and sliced Provolone cheese.

3. Add the other bread quarters, hummus side in, to create two sandwiches.

4. Butter the outside of the bread and toast until the cheese is melty. Serve and enjoy!

Barbecue Chicken Sandwich

Ingredients

- » Butter, as needed
- » 2 white bread slices
- » 1 slice cheddar cheese
- » 1 slice smoked Gouda cheese
- » 1 cup cooked chicken
- » ⅓ cup red onion, sliced
- » 2 tablespoons barbecue sauce
- » Barbecue chips, for serving

Serves 1

1. Butter one side of each slice of bread.

2. Add the cheddar and Gouda cheeses, chicken, onion, and barbecue sauce to the unbuttered side of one slice.

3. Top with the other bread slice, butter side up. Close the iron, trim as needed, and toast. Serve with barbecue chips and enjoy!

Toasted BLT

Serves 1

Ingredients

» Butter, as needed
» 2 Italian bread slices
» 1 tablespoon mayonnaise
» 1 tomato, sliced
» 2 slices cooked bacon
» Lettuce leaves, for serving

1. Butter one side of each slice of bread.

2. Spread the unbuttered sides with mayo and add some tomato and bacon.

3. Top with the other bread slice, butter side up. Close the iron, trim as needed, and toast.

4. Slide the sandwich out of the iron and wrap in a lettuce leaf. Put lettuce inside the sandwich if you'd like, and enjoy!

Cheese & Onion Puffs

Serves 2

Ingredients
» 4 puff pastries
» 4 onion slices
» Handful shredded Swiss cheese
» Handful shredded cheddar cheese
» Salt and pepper, to taste

1. Generously grease an iron.

2. Add pastries inside the iron. Add the onion slices, cheeses, salt, and pepper.

3. A second pastry piece goes on top; seal the edges. Close the iron and toast (if dough oozes out, just trim it off).

4. When it looks like a little golden pillow, it's done. Enjoy!

Inside-Out Jalapeño Poppers

Serves 1

Ingredients

- » 1 cup Corn Flakes cereal
- » Salt and pepper, to taste
- » Garlic powder, to taste
- » Cumin, to taste
- » 2 slices whole grain bread
- » 1 tablespoon cream cheese, softened
- » 1 slice cheddar cheese
- » 1 roasted red bell pepper, chopped
- » 1 jalapeño pepper

1. Grease an iron.
2. Crush the cereal; stir in the seasonings.
3. Coat a bread slice with cooking spray; dip it into the crumbs. Set the coated side face down in the iron.
4. Spread with a nice thick layer of cream cheese. Add the cheddar and peppers.
5. Slice the jalapeño, remove the seeds, and add it to the iron.
6. Spread cream cheese on a second bread slice; coat in breadcrumbs and dip the other side in cream cheese.
7. Set the bread on the peppers, crumb side up. Close the iron and trim; toast until the cheese is melty. Enjoy!

Cobb Sandwich

Ingredients

- » Butter, as needed
- » 2 whole wheat bread slices
- » 1 boneless, skinless chicken breast, cooked and sliced
- » 2 slices cooked bacon (crispy)
- » 1 avocado, sliced
- » 1 egg, hardboiled
- » Shredded Gouda cheese, to taste
- » Blue cheese crumbles, to taste

1. Butter one side of each slice of bread.
2. Layer all the ingredients between both bread slices and place the sandwich in a panini press. Toast until warm. Enjoy!

Ultimate Greek Sandwich

Ingredients

- » Butter, as needed
- » 2 sourdough bread slices
- » 1 tablespoon original-flavored hummus
- » 1 slice Provolone cheese
- » ⅓ cup red onion, sliced
- » 2 slices roasted deli turkey
- » ⅓ cup roasted red peppers, sliced
- » 3 slices cucumber
- » ⅓ cup Kalamata olives, sliced
- » Feta cheese, crumbled, to taste

1. Butter one side of each slice of bread.
2. Spread the hummus on the unbuttered side of the bead.
3. Layer the remaining ingredients between slices and toast in a panini press.
4. Serve warm and enjoy!

Classic Italian

Serves 1

Ingredients

- » Butter, as needed
- » 2 sourdough bread slices
- » 1 slice Provolone cheese
- » 2 slices mozzarella cheese
- » 3 slices deli Genoa salami
- » 3 slices deli ham
- » ¼ cup Giardiniera
- » 2 tablespoons green and Kalamata olives, sliced
- » 3 pepperoncini, sliced

Butter one side of each slice of bread. Layer all the ingredients between bread slices and toast in a greased panini press. Enjoy!

Spicy Sausage Sandwich

Serves 1

Ingredients

- » Butter, as needed
- » 2 rye bread slices
- » 1 slice Gouda cheese
- » 1 slice Chipotle cheddar cheese
- » 1 slice Muenster cheese
- » ⅓ cup green bell pepper, sliced
- » ⅓ cup onion, sliced
- » 1 cooked Italian sausage, sliced

Butter one side of each slice of bread. Layer all the remaining ingredients and toast. Enjoy!

Cheesy Spinach Calzone

Ingredients

» 1 package refrigerated pizza dough
» 1 cup frozen spinach, thawed and drained
» 1 onion, sliced
» 1 bell pepper, sliced
» 2 mushrooms, sliced
» 1 teaspoon minced garlic
» 1 cup alfredo sauce
» 1 cup shredded Provolone cheese
» Salt and black pepper, to taste

Serves 1

1. Grease an iron.

2. Roll the dough thin and cut it to fit the iron; press one piece inside.

3. Add the remaining ingredients and top with another dough piece.

4. Close the iron and toast until the dough is toasted on both sides. Serve and enjoy!

Stuffed Portobello Bake

Serves 2

Ingredients

- » 2 portobello mushroom caps
- » 2 tablespoons mayonnaise
- » 2 tablespoons onions, chopped
- » 1 can tiny shrimp, drained
- » Fresh basil, to taste
- » ⅓ cup shredded Parmesan cheese
- » 2 tablespoons breadcrumbs
- » Olive oil, to taste

1. Remove each mushroom's stem and gills.

2. Grease an iron; set the mushroom caps inside.

3. Spread the cavities with a little mayo. Toss on onions, shrimp, and basil. Top with a handful of cheese and breadcrumbs. Add a drizzle of oil and close the iron.

4. Toast until the breadcrumbs are crunchy. Serve and enjoy!

Spinach Artichoke Sandwich

Serves 1

Ingredients

» 1 tablespoon canned artichoke hearts
» Butter, as needed
» 2 sourdough bread slices
» 1 tablespoon frozen chopped spinach
» 1 tablespoon mayonnaise
» 1 teaspoon garlic powder
» Salt and black pepper, to taste
» ½ cup shredded mozzarella cheese
» 1 tablespoon shredded Parmesan cheese

1. Thaw and squeeze excess moisture from the spinach and drain and chop the artichokes.

2. Butter one side of each slice of bread.

3. Mix equal parts spinach, artichokes, and mayo; season with the garlic powder, salt, and pepper and spread on the unbuttered side of the bread.

4. Add the cheeses and toast in a panini press. Enjoy!

Pesto Panini

Serves 1

Ingredients

» Butter, as needed
» 2 slices Italian bread
» 2 tablespoons pesto
» 1 tablespoon fire-roasted tomatoes, drained
» 2 slices salami
» ⅓ cup shredded mozzarella cheese

Butter one side of each slice of bread. Layer all the ingredients inside, toast until melty, and enjoy!

The Peachy-Keen Sandwich

Serves 1

1. Butter one side of each part of the roll.
2. Spread the mustard and preserves on the inside of the roll.
3. Layer the remaining ingredients between the roll halves and toast both sides in a panini press. Enjoy!

Ingredients
- » Butter, as needed
- » 1 ciabatta roll, split
- » 1 tablespoon whole grain Dijon mustard
- » 1 tablespoon peach preserves
- » 2 slices Canadian bacon
- » 1 peach, sliced
- » ½ cup shredded fontina cheese
- » Fresh thyme, to taste

Fresh from the Garden Sandwich

Serves 1

Ingredients
- » Butter, as needed
- » 2 whole wheat bread slices
- » 1 tablespoon cream cheese, softened
- » 1 teaspoon fresh chives, chopped
- » ⅓ cup red onion, finely chopped
- » 1 tomato, sliced
- » 1 teaspoon fresh basil, chopped
- » Salt and pepper, to taste

1. Butter one side of each slice of bread.
2. Combine the cream cheese, chives, and onion and spread the mixture on the unbuttered side of the bread.
3. Layer the remaining ingredients between slices and toast in a panini press. Enjoy!

Nacho Grilled Cheese

Serves 1

Ingredients

- » Butter, as needed
- » 2 cheese bread slices
- » 2 slices pepper jack cheese
- » ⅓ cup black beans, drained and rinsed
- » ⅓ cup black olives, sliced
- » ⅓ cup green onion, chopped
- » 1 avocado, sliced
- » 1 tablespoon salsa
- » 4 nacho cheese-flavored tortilla chips
- » Sour cream, for dipping

1. Butter one side of each slice of bread.
2. Layer the remaining ingredients between bread slices and toast in a panini press.
3. Serve warm with sour cream for dipping.

Apple Gruyère Sandwich

Serves 1

Ingredients

- » Butter, as needed
- » 2 multigrain bread slices
- » 1 tablespoon mayonnaise
- » 1 crisp red apple, thinly sliced
- » ½ cup shredded Gruyère cheese
- » ¼ cup fresh arugula

1. Butter one side of each slice of bread.
2. Spread mayonnaise on the unbuttered side of the bread.
3. Layer the remaining ingredients between slices and toast in a panini press.
4. Serve and enjoy!

Parmesan Crisps

Serves 4

Ingredients

- » 1 ½ cups shredded Parmesan cheese
- » 1 tablespoon flour
- » 2 teaspoons fresh basil or oregano, chopped
- » Marinara sauce, for dipping

1. Lightly grease your waffle iron and preheat it (if your iron has a browning control setting, set it on medium-high).

2. Toss the cheese with the flour until coated. Then stir in the basil.

3. Make a mound of the cheese mixture (about 2 tablespoons) on each section of the iron. Close the lid and cook until they're brown and baked to beautiful perfection. (These will lift easily out of the iron, and the little cheesy bits that get left behind are yummy, too.)

4. Dip into marinara sauce for extra Italian flair if you'd like. Enjoy!

Field of Greens Sandwich

Serves 1

Ingredients
- » Butter, as needed
- » 2 multigrain bread slices
- » 2 slices deli roasted turkey
- » ½ cup fresh arugula
- » 1 avocado, sliced
- » Goat cheese, crumbled, to taste

Butter one side of each slice of bread. Layer the remaining ingredients in between the bread slices and toast in a panini press. Enjoy!

Prosciutto and Brie Sandwich

Serves 1

Ingredients
- » Butter, as needed
- » 2 sourdough bread slices
- » 2 slices Brie cheese
- » 2 slices prosciutto
- » ⅓ cup fresh arugula

Butter one side of each slice of bread. Layer the remaining ingredients in between the bread slices and toast in a panini press. Enjoy!

Broccoli Cheddar Sandwich

Serves 1

Ingredients
- » Butter, as needed
- » 1 ciabatta roll, split
- » 2 slices sharp cheddar cheese
- » 1 tablespoon honey mustard
- » 2 slices deli smoked turkey breast
- » ½ cup broccoli, steamed
- » Salt and pepper, to taste

Butter one side of each piece of the roll. Layer the remaining ingredients in between the roll halves and toast in a panini press. Enjoy!

Pear and Bacon Sandwich

Serves 1

Ingredients
- » Butter, as needed
- » 2 multigrain bread slices
- » 1 tablespoon fig jam
- » 2 slices cheddar cheese
- » 3 strips cooked bacon (crispy)
- » 1 pear, thinly sliced

1. Butter one side of each slice of bread.

2. Spread jam on the unbuttered sides of the bread.

3. Layer all the remaining ingredients between the slices and toast in a panini press. Enjoy!

Beer-Battered Shrimp

Serves 8

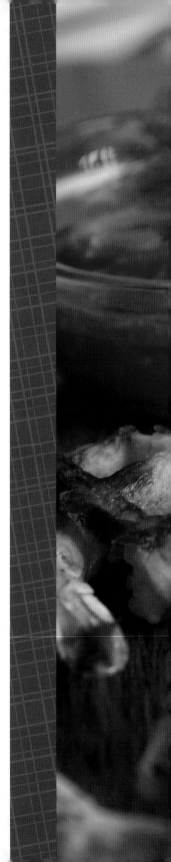

Ingredients
» 1 (12 ounce) can beer
» 2 cups flour
» 1 teaspoon garlic powder
» 1½ teaspoons salt
» 1 teaspoon black pepper
» ¾ to 1 teaspoon cayenne pepper
» About 2 pounds peeled and deveined cooked shrimp, thawed
» Lemon juice and favorite dipping sauce, for serving (optional)

1. Whisk together the beer, flour, garlic powder, salt, black pepper, and cayenne pepper until smooth.

2. Preheat and grease your waffle iron.

3. Dunk the shrimp in the batter and remove the excess. Arrange several shrimp on the iron and close the lid.

4. Cook until the batter is light golden brown and no longer doughy.

5. Peek in on them every now and then to see how they're doing (they may need to cook for several minutes after the indicator light comes on).

6. Drizzle with lemon juice and dunk into your favorite sauce, if desired.

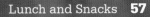

The Sizzling Jalapeño Crunch

Serves 1

Ingredients

- » Butter, as needed
- » 2 sourdough bread slices
- » 2 slices sharp cheddar cheese
- » 1 tomato, sliced
- » Handful barbecue potato chips
- » 2 pickled jalapeños, sliced
- » 2 strips cooked bacon (crispy)

Butter one side of each slice of bread. Layer all the ingredients between the bread slices and toast in a panini press. Enjoy!

Brussels Sprout Melt

Serves 1

Ingredients

- » Butter, as needed
- » 2 whole grain bread slices
- » ⅓ cup stemless Brussels sprouts, thinly sliced
- » 2 teaspoons garlic, minced
- » 1 teaspoon balsamic vinegar
- » 1 slice Havarti cheese
- » Salt and pepper, to taste

1. Sauté the Brussels sprouts and garlic; add the salt, pepper, and balsamic vinegar.

2. Butter one side of each slice of bread.

3. Layer all the ingredients between the bread slices and toast in a panini press. Enjoy!

Turkey Pesto Sandwich

Serves 1

Ingredients
- » Butter, as needed
- » 6-inch French bread loaf, split
- » 2 tablespoons basil pesto
- » 2 slices mozzarella cheese
- » 1 avocado, sliced
- » 5 slices deli roast turkey
- » 1 tomato, sliced
- » Black pepper, to taste

Butter one side of each slice of bread. Layer all the ingredients between the bread slices and toast in a panini press. Enjoy!

Five-Cheese Melt

Serves 1

Ingredients
- » Butter, as needed
- » Italian bread slices
- » Shredded Parmesan cheese, to taste
- » 2 slices Provolone cheese
- » 2 slices fresh mozzarella cheese
- » Shredded fontina cheese, to taste
- » ⅓ cup cheese curds

1. Butter and sprinkle Parmesan on one side of each slice of bread.
2. Layer all remaining cheeses between bread slices and toast in a panini press. Enjoy!

Cheese-Studded Waffles

Serves 8

1. Whisk together the butter, buttermilk, and eggs until well combined. Add the mashed potatoes and chives. Stir gently until blended.

2. In a separate bowl, stir together all the dry ingredients and the cheese. Add this mixture to the buttermilk mixture and stir, but don't over-mix (you just want the dry ingredients to disappear).

3. Preheat and lightly grease your waffle iron.

4. Drop the potatoes in ⅓-cup mounds, close the lid, and bake until golden brown and slightly crispy (they may need to cook for a few minutes after the iron's indicator light comes on).

5. Garnish and serve any way you'd like. Some extra chives for color? Why not!

WHY WAFFLE IT?
These potatoes are crunchy on the outside, soft on the inside. It's potato perfection!

Ingredients

» ¼ cup butter, melted
» ¼ cup buttermilk
» 2 eggs
» 2 cups leftover mashed potatoes
» 2 tablespoons fresh chives, chopped
» ½ cup flour
» ½ teaspoon baking powder
» ½ teaspoon salt
» ½ teaspoon pepper
» ¼ teaspoon baking soda
» ¼ teaspoon garlic powder
» 1 cup shredded Colby Jack cheese

Waffle-Style Corn Dogs

Serves 10

1. Stir together the dry ingredients.

2. Mix in the egg and 1 cup evaporated milk until well blended, adding the remaining ¼ cup milk to reach dipping consistency, if needed. Transfer the batter to a tall drinking glass.

3. Preheat and lightly grease your waffle iron.

4. Pat the hot dogs dry and insert a bamboo skewer lengthwise through the center of each. Dip each hot dog into the batter, swirl, and lift.

5. You'll want a fairly thin coating of batter, so gently remove excess.

6. Place a couple of the hot dogs on the hot iron, set the lid down gently, and cook until no longer doughy. Enjoy immediately.

TRY THIS INSTEAD

If you don't have skewers, you can just slice 8 to 10 small hot dogs and stir them into the batter. Pour the batter in batches onto the greased iron, close the lid, and cook until done.

Ingredients

» 1 cup flour
» ½ cup yellow cornmeal
» 1 tablespoon sugar
» 1 tablespoon baking powder
» 1 teaspoon salt
» ½ teaspoon dry mustard
» ¼ teaspoon paprika
» ¼ teaspoon black pepper
» 1 egg
» 1 to 1 ¼ cups evaporated milk
» 10 small or regular hot dogs

Faux Fry Hodge Podge

Servings Vary

1. Cut the veggies into desired shapes that are all about the same thickness. Remove excess moisture by blotting with paper towels; set aside.

2. Stir together the milk, vinegar, oil, flour, baking powder, salt, cayenne pepper, garlic salt, and dill weed until well blended.

3. Grease and preheat your waffle iron (if your iron has a browning control setting, set it on high).

4. Dip the veggies partway into the batter and remove any excess.

5. Place them on the hot iron, close the lid, and cook until golden brown.

6. Enjoy immediately. Serve with dipping sauce of your choice.

WHY WAFFLE IT?

No deep fryer oil splatters messing up your nice clean kitchen. Without all that oil, this snack is healthier, too!

Ingredients

» Assorted fresh veggies (I used mushrooms, zucchini, dill pickles, onion, and bell pepper)

» 1 cup milk

» 2 tablespoons distilled white vinegar

» 1 ½ tablespoons vegetable oil

» 1 ¼ to 1 ½ cups flour

» 1 teaspoon baking powder

» 1 teaspoon salt

» ¼ teaspoon cayenne pepper

» 1 teaspoon garlic salt

» ½ teaspoon dill weed

» Dipping sauce, for serving

Dinner

◇◇◇◇◇◇◇◇◇◇◇◇◇◇◇◇◇◇◇◇◇◇◇◇◇◇◇◇◇◇◇◇◇◇◇◇◇◇

The next time you're debating what to make for dinner, look no further than these delicious, crispy waffled entrées. Almost any meal you can think of can be waffled—turn the page to see some crunchy, flavor-packed options, from sandwiches to lasagna!

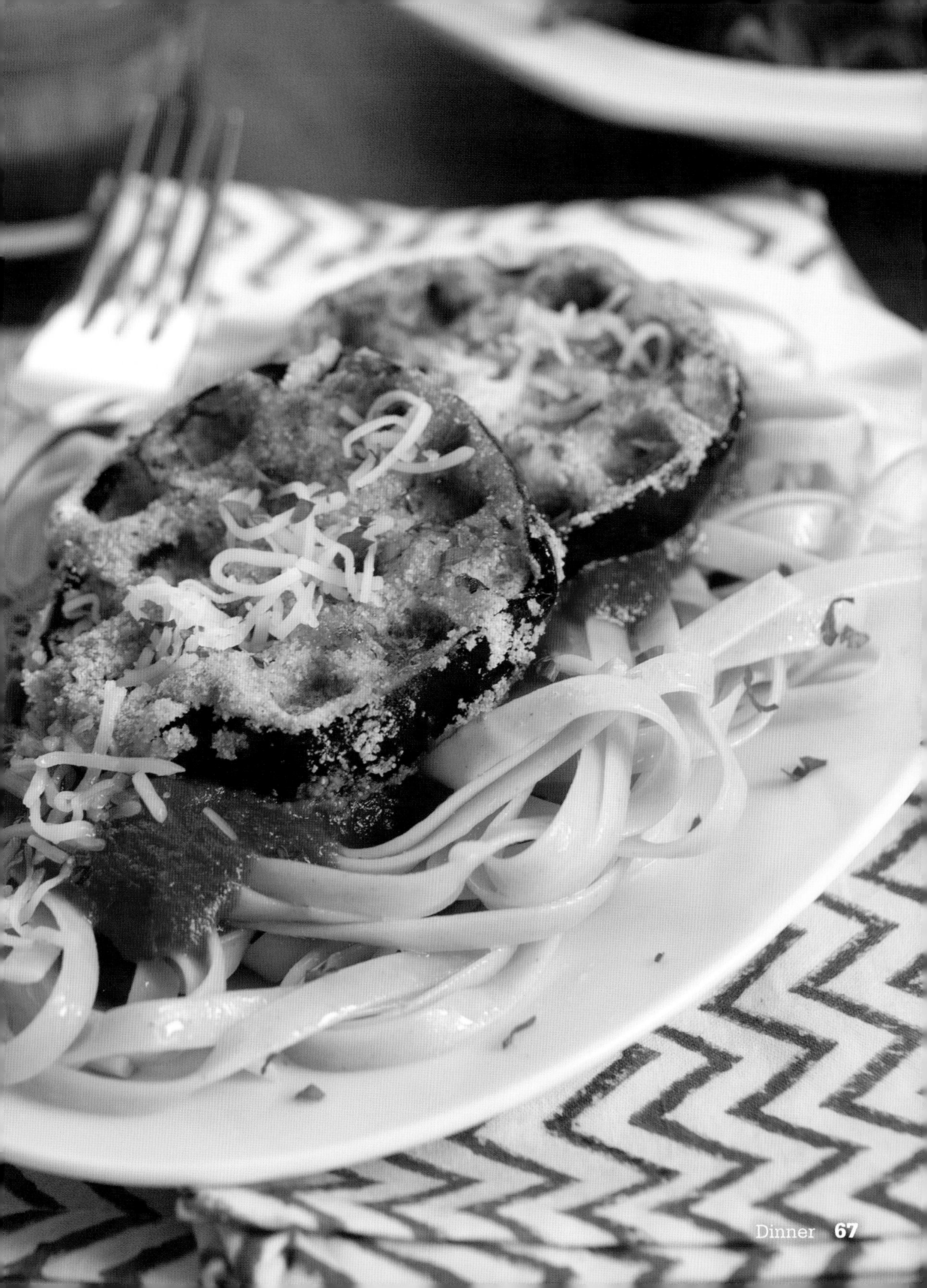

Pizza Waffles

Serves 8

1. Preheat and lightly grease your waffle iron.

2. Simply cut a pocket into the side of each biscuit and stuff with topping ingredients; press the edges to seal the toppings safely inside.

3. Put a few on the iron; set the lid down gently, and cook until toasty brown, pressing down lightly on the handle occasionally so the dough in the front is cooked (use a hot pad).

4. Serve with a side of pizza sauce for dipping if you'd like.

Ingredients

» 1 (16.3 ounce) tube refrigerated Grands Flaky Layers Buttermilk biscuits

» Pizza sauce, as needed, plus more for dipping

» Pizza toppings (I used mini pepperoni, green bell pepper, mushrooms, and chives), as needed

» Shredded cheese (I used an Italian cheese blend), as needed

Hawaiian Waffle Quesadillas

Servings Vary

Ingredients

» Flour tortillas
» Shredded cheese (I used a Mexican cheese blend), as needed
» Crushed pineapple, drained, as needed
» 1 red onion, chopped
» Canadian bacon slices or cooked, crumbled bacon, as needed
» Barbecue sauce, plus more for dipping, as needed
» Sour cream, for dipping, as needed

1. Lightly grease your waffle iron, but don't preheat it.

2. Lay one tortilla on the cold iron. Add thin layers of cheese, pineapple, onion, and Canadian bacon.

3. Drizzle with a little barbecue sauce and set another tortilla on top.

4. Plug in the iron, close the lid, and cook until the little pockets made by the iron are light golden brown.

5. Serve with extra barbecue sauce and maybe a little sour cream for good measure.

Monte Cristo

1. Preheat your waffle iron.

2. For each sandwich, spread the cut sides of a Bagel Thin with mustard and mayo.

3. To the coated side of one half, add thin layers of turkey, ham, and cheese. Place the other bagel half on top, cut side down.

4. In a small bowl, beat together the egg and milk until well combined.

Ingredients
- » 4 Bagel Thins
- » Mustard, to taste
- » Mayonnaise, to taste
- » 4 slices deli sliced turkey
- » 4 slices deli sliced ham
- » 4 slices Swiss cheese
- » 1 egg
- » About ½ cup milk

5. Dip both sides of one sandwich in the egg mixture and place it on the hot iron. Close the lid and press down lightly on the handle.

6. Cook until toasted to your liking. Repeat with the remaining sandwiches. Enjoy!

Leftover Spaghetti Melt

Serves 1

Ingredients

» Butter, as needed
» Garlic salt, to taste
» 2 Italian bread slices
» 1 cup prepared spaghetti with sauce
» ½ cup shredded Romano cheese
» 2 teaspoons Italian seasoning

1. Butter and sprinkle garlic salt on one side of each slice of bread.
2. Layer all remaining ingredients between bread slices and toast in the panini press. Enjoy!

The Cordon Bleu

Serves 1

Ingredients

» Butter, as needed
» 2 sourdough bread slices
» 1 tablespoon mayonnaise
» 1 tablespoon Dijon mustard
» 1 boneless, skinless chicken breast, cooked and sliced
» 2 slices prosciutto
» ½ cup shredded Gruyère cheese
» 1 teaspoon fresh thyme

1. Butter one side of each slice of bread.
2. Combine the mayo and mustard.
3. Layer all the remaining ingredients between the bread slices, add the combined sauces, and toast in a panini press. Enjoy!

Barbecue Chicken Melt

Serves 1

Ingredients

- » Butter, as needed
- » 2 sourdough bread slices
- » 1 boneless, skinless chicken breast, cooked and shredded
- » 1 tablespoon barbecue sauce
- » ⅓ cup red onion, sliced
- » 2 slices Provolone cheese
- » 2 teaspoons fresh cilantro, chopped

1. Butter one side of each slice of bread.
2. Combine the shredded chicken and the barbecue sauce.
3. Layer all the ingredients between the bread slices and toast. Enjoy!

Roast Beef Sandwich **Serves 1**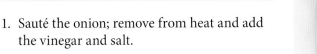

Ingredients

- » ⅓ cup red onion, sliced
- » 1 tablespoon balsamic vinegar
- » Salt, to taste
- » Butter, as needed
- » 2 multigrain bread slices
- » 1 tablespoon mayonnaise
- » 1 tablespoon prepared horseradish
- » 5 leaves fresh baby spinach
- » 2 slices deli roast beef
- » 2 teaspoons blue cheese crumbles

1. Sauté the onion; remove from heat and add the vinegar and salt.
2. Butter one side of each slice of bread.
3. Combine the mayo and horseradish and spread on the unbuttered side of the bread.
4. Layer all the ingredients between bread slices and toast in a panini press. Serve and enjoy!

Lasagna Waffles

Serves 6

Ingredients
- » 6 uncooked lasagna noodles
- » Vegetable oil, as needed
- » ½ cup ricotta cheese
- » ½ teaspoon minced garlic
- » 1 egg yolk, beaten
- » ½ teaspoon salt
- » ¼ teaspoon pepper
- » 1 (6 ounce) Italian sausage, cooked, drained, and crumbled
- » ½ (10 ounce) package frozen chopped spinach, thawed and squeezed dry
- » ½ cup shredded cheese (I used Colby Jack), plus more for sprinkling
- » Marinara sauce, as needed, plus more for serving

1. Cook the noodles according to package directions until nearly done; drain the pasta and drizzle with a little oil. Stir together the ricotta cheese, garlic, egg yolk, salt, and pepper.

2. Preheat and grease your waffle iron.

3. Lay the noodles side by side on a flat surface. Divide the ricotta cheese mixture, sausage, spinach, and shredded cheese evenly among the noodles, covering only half of each noodle with the mixture. Drizzle each with a little marinara sauce. Fold the plain half of each noodle over the filling.

4. Carefully move one or two of the filled noodles to the iron and set the lid down gently. Cook until the noodles are just beginning to brown and the filling is bubbly.

5. Remove from the iron and serve with extra marinara sauce and a little extra cheese if you'd like. Enjoy!

Toasted Caprese Sandwich

Serves 1

Ingredients

- » 1 boneless, skinless chicken breast
- » 1 teaspoon garlic powder
- » 1 teaspoon Italian seasoning
- » Black pepper, to taste
- » Butter, as needed
- » 2 Italian bread slices
- » 3 slices fresh mozzarella cheese
- » 1 tomato, sliced
- » 1 tablespoon fresh basil, chopped
- » Balsamic glaze, for dipping

1. Cook the chicken in a skillet and season with the garlic powder, Italian seasoning, and black pepper.
2. Butter one side of each slice of bread.
3. Layer all the ingredients between bread slices and toast in a panini press. Serve with balsamic glaze for dipping.

Sassy Shrimp Sammy

Serves 1

Ingredients

- » Butter, as needed
- » 2 sourdough bread slices
- » 2 tablespoons cream cheese, softened
- » Sliced green onion
- » Garlic salt
- » 1 tablespoon soy sauce
- » 2 teaspoons Worcestershire sauce
- » Black pepper, to taste
- » 1 cup cooked shrimp

1. Butter one side of each slice of bread.
2. Combine the cream cheese, green onion, garlic salt, soy sauce, Worcestershire sauce, and black pepper and spread on the unbuttered side of the bread.
3. Add the shrimp to the sandwich and toast. Serve and enjoy.

Gouda Mushroom Melt

Ingredients

- » 2 portobello mushrooms, sliced
- » 1 teaspoon garlic, minced
- » Butter, as needed
- » 2 whole wheat bread slices
- » 2 tablespoons cream cheese, softened
- » ⅓ cup fresh baby spinach
- » ½ cup shredded Gouda cheese
- » 1 tablespoon fresh chives, chopped
- » Salt and black pepper, to taste

1. Sauté the mushrooms and garlic.
2. Butter one side of each slice of bread.
3. Spread cream cheese on the unbuttered side of the bread.
4. Layer all the ingredients between slices and toast in a panini press. Enjoy!

Toasted Turkey Sandwich

Ingredients

- » Butter, as needed
- » 2 sourdough bread slices
- » 1 tablespoon port wine cheese spread
- » 2 slices Provolone cheese
- » 2 slices deli roast turkey breast
- » 1 tomato, sliced
- » 2 slices cooked bacon (crispy)
- » Black pepper, to taste

1. Butter one side of each slice of bread.
2. Spread the port wine cheese on the unbuttered side of the bread.
3. Layer all the remaining ingredients and toast in a panini press. When warm, serve and enjoy!

Eggplant Parm

Serves 4

Ingredients

- ¼ cup flour
- ½ teaspoon pepper
- 2 teaspoons salt, divided
- 1 egg, beaten
- ¼ cup water
- ½ cup dry Italian bread crumbs
- ¼ cup cornmeal
- 1 tablespoon Parmesan cheese, grated
- 1 eggplant, sliced into ½-inch rounds
- Cooked pasta, as needed
- Pasta sauce, as needed
- Shredded cheese (I used an Italian Cheese blend), as needed

1. In a bowl, stir together the flour, pepper, and 1 teaspoon of the salt.

2. In another bowl, whisk together the egg and water until well blended.

3. In a third bowl, combine the breadcrumbs, cornmeal, Parmesan cheese, and remaining 1 teaspoon salt; stir to blend.

4. Preheat and grease your waffle iron.

5. Dip both sides of the eggplant rounds into the flour mixture, then the egg, and then the bread crumb mixture. Arrange a few of them on the hot iron, set the lid down gently, and cook until toasty brown. Repeat with the remaining rounds (they may need to cook for a few minutes after the iron's indicator light comes on).

6. Serve with hot cooked pasta, sauce, and shredded cheese.

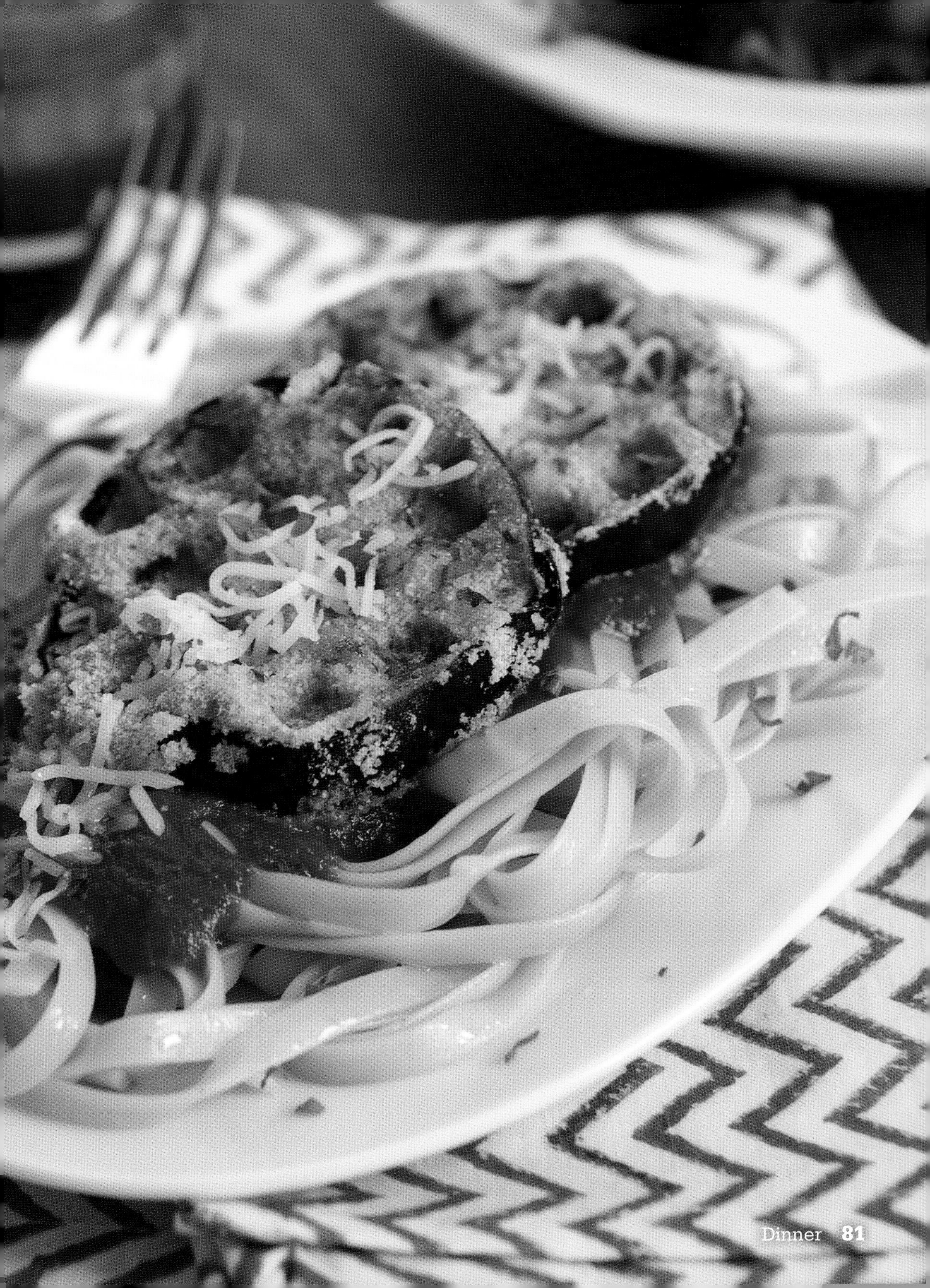

The Frenchman

Serves 1

Ingredients

» Butter, as needed
» 6-inch French bread loaf, split
» 2 slices Gruyère cheese
» 2 slices deli ham
» 2 sweet gherkins, sliced
» 1 tablespoon Dijon mustard
» 2 teaspoons dried tarragon
» Black pepper, to taste

Butter one side of each slice of bread. Layer all the ingredients in between bread halves and toast. Enjoy!

The Oktober-Feast

Serves 1

Ingredients

» Butter, as needed
» Pretzel roll, split
» 3 slices Muenster cheese
» 1 tablespoon honey mustard
» 1 brat, cooked and sliced in half lengthwise
» 1 tablespoon coleslaw
» 1 teaspoon carraway seeds

Butter one side of each slice of roll. Layer all the ingredients in between slices and toast to perfection. Enjoy!

French Onion Steak Sandwich

Serves 1

Ingredients

- » 5-ounce top sirloin steak
- » Garlic salt
- » ⅓ cup yellow onion, sliced
- » 1 potato, thinly sliced
- » Salt and black pepper, to taste
- » Butter, as needed
- » 2 French bread slices
- » 1 slice Provolone cheese
- » ⅓ cup green onion, sliced

1. Cook and season the steak to your liking then thinly slice it.
2. Sauté the onion and potato; season with salt and pepper.
3. Butter one side of each slice of bread.
4. Layer all the ingredients between bread slices and toast. Enjoy!

Guacamole Galore

Serves 1

Ingredients

- » Butter, as needed
- » 2 sourdough bread slices
- » 2 tablespoons guacamole
- » 3 slices cooked bacon (crispy)
- » ⅓ cup shredded Colby Jack cheese
- » Tortilla chips, crumbled

1. Butter one side of each slice of bread.
2. Spread the guacamole on the unbuttered side of the bread.
3. Layer remaining ingredients between bread slices and toast. Serve and enjoy!

Waffled Crabby Patties

Serves 6

1. Place the crabmeat in a bowl and gently break it apart.

2. In a separate bowl, whisk together the egg white, mayo, mustard, seasoning, lemon juice, Worcestershire sauce, and salt.

3. Add the egg mixture to the crab meat and stir gently without over-mixing. Toss in the breadcrumbs and parsley; mix gently.

4. Cover with plastic wrap and refrigerate for 1 hour.

5. Preheat and lightly grease your waffle iron.

6. Drop heaping tablespoons of the chilled crab mixture onto the hot iron. Close the lid and cook a few minutes until nicely browned.

7. Serve with fruit salsa or your favorite seafood dipping sauce. Enjoy!

WAFFLE THIS INSTEAD

How about making tuna patties?
Just replace crabmeat with 1 (7 ounce) pouch of tuna. Mix and cook as directed above.

Ingredients

» 1 (8 ounce) package imitation crab meat

» 1 egg white

» 2 tablespoons mayonnaise

» ¾ teaspoon Dijon mustard

» ½ to ¾ teaspoon Old Bay seasoning

» ½ teaspoon lemon juice

» ¼ teaspoon Worcestershire sauce

» ¼ teaspoon salt

» ½ cup plus 2 tablespoons fresh breadcrumbs from soft white sandwich bread

» 1 ½ teaspoons fresh parsley, chopped

» Fruit salsa or dipping sauce, for serving

Stromboli Sandwich

Ingredients

- » Butter, as needed
- » 6-inch French bread loaf, split
- » 2 tablespoons pizza sauce
- » ⅓ cup shredded mozzarella cheese
- » 2 slices Genoa salami
- » 2 slices deli Capicola ham
- » 1 red onion, sliced
- » 3 pepperoncini, sliced
- » 1 tablespoon sun-dried tomatoes
- » 1 tablespoon shredded Parmesan cheese

1. Butter one side of each slice of bread.
2. Spread pizza sauce on the unbuttered side of the bread.
3. Layer the remaining ingredients between slices and toast. Enjoy!

Classic Reuben

Ingredients

- » Butter, as needed
- » 2 slices marbled rye bread
- » ½ cup sauerkraut, drained
- » 3 slices deli corned beef
- » ⅓ cup Swiss cheese, shredded
- » 1 tablespoon thousand island dressing

Butter one side of each slice of bread. Layer all the ingredients in between slices and toast to perfection. Enjoy!

Mac and Cheese Sammy

Serves 1

Ingredients

- » Butter, as needed
- » 2 Italian bread slices
- » 1 cup prepared macaroni and cheese
- » 2 slices pancetta, pan fried
- » Shredded Asiago cheese, to taste

Butter one side of each slice of bread. Layer all the ingredients in between slices and toast to perfection. Enjoy!

The Buffalo Ranch

Serves 1

Ingredients

- » Butter, as needed
- » 2 sourdough bread slices
- » 2 tablespoons buffalo sauce
- » 1 slice Provolone cheese
- » 2 breaded chicken tenders, cooked
- » 1 tablespoon ranch dressing
- » Blue cheese crumbles, to taste
- » 1 teaspoon fresh chives, chopped

Butter one side of each slice of bread. Layer all the ingredients in between slices and toast to perfection. Enjoy!

Thanksgiving Leftovers

 **Serves 6**

1. Preheat and lightly grease your waffle iron.

2. Stir together the stuffing, celery, turkey, and dried cranberries until well blended. If your mixture is dry, stir in a bit of chicken broth or water (you want it to hold together just a bit).

3. Pack an even layer of the stuffing mixture onto your iron (and really fill those corners, too).

4. Close the lid and cook until nicely browned and crisp. Serve and enjoy!

You can waffle your leftover mashed potatoes, too!

(See recipe on page 60.)

WAFFLING TIP

Don't cover the dividers in your iron with stuffing–the waffles are easier to remove if you have smaller portions. Customize your stuffing by adding chopped fresh mushrooms, pine nuts, or extra herbs if you'd like. Serve with cranberry sauce or gravy, too!

Ingredients

» 4 cups leftover stuffing (or prepared Stovetop Stuffing)

» ½ cup celery, finely diced

» 1 cup cooked turkey, shredded or diced

» ½ cup dried cranberries

» Chicken broth (optional)

Chicken & Waffles Sandwich

Serves 1

Ingredients

- » Butter, as needed
- » 2 frozen waffles, thawed
- » 1 breaded chicken tender, cooked
- » Hot sauce, to taste
- » ⅓ cup shredded sharp cheddar cheese
- » Cajun seasoning, to taste
- » 1 tablespoon green onion, chopped
- » Honey or maple syrup, for dipping

1. Butter one side of each waffle.
2. Layer ingredients between waffles and toast until crispy.
3. Serve with honey or maple syrup for dipping. Enjoy!

Chipotle Mushroom Melt

Serves 1

Ingredients

- » 2 baby bella mushrooms, sliced
- » Butter, as needed
- » 6-inch French bread loaf, split
- » 1 tablespoon cream cheese, softened
- » ½ cup chipotle peppers in adobo sauce, sliced
- » ½ cup shredded cheddar cheese
- » 2 teaspoons fresh cilantro, chopped

1. Sauté the mushrooms.
2. Butter one side of the bread loaf, and spread the cream cheese on the unbuttered side.
3. Layer all the other ingredients between halves and toast to perfection. Enjoy!

Dill Corned Beef Sandwich

Serves 1

Ingredients

- » Butter, as needed
- » 2 sourdough bread slices
- » 1 tablespoon sour cream
- » 1 tablespoon mayonnaise
- » 2 slices deli corned beef
- » 1 tablespoon dill pickle relish
- » ⅓ cup dill-flavored Monterey Jack cheese, shredded
- » 1 tablespoon green onion, finely chopped

1. Butter one side of each slice of bread.

2. Mix equal amounts of sour cream and mayo and spread the mixture on the unbuttered side of the bread.

3. Layer remaining ingredients and toast. Enjoy!

Chicken Parm Melt

Serves 1

Ingredients

- » Butter, as needed
- » 2 sourdough bread slices
- » 2 tablespoons marinara sauce
- » 2 breaded chicken tenders, cooked and sliced
- » ⅓ cup shredded mozzarella cheese
- » 1 tablespoon shredded Parmesan cheese
- » 1 teaspoon fresh basil
- » Black pepper, to taste

1. Butter one side of each slice of bread.

2. Spread marinara sauce on the unbuttered side of the bread.

3. Layer remaining ingredients between slices and toast to crispy perfection. Enjoy!

Garden Veggie Calzones

Serves 6

1. Grease your waffle iron, but don't preheat it.

2. In a large bowl, mix the carrots, mushrooms, zucchini, bell pepper, onion, garlic salt, and pepper.

3. Thinly roll out the pizza dough and cut it into pieces to fit on the iron.

4. Set one piece on the cold iron. Place about half the veggie mixture and half the cheese in a thin, even layer over the dough. Add basil and set a second piece of dough on top.

5. Set the lid down gently and plug in the iron. Cook until nicely browned, pressing down lightly on the handle occasionally so the dough in the front gets done.

6. Serve with marinara sauce and enjoy!

SWITCH IT UP!

Switch out any of the filling ingredients with your favorites. Want meat? Add it. Cheese only? No problem. Asparagus in the spring, squash in the fall? You bet—waffle them all!

Ingredients

- » ¼ cup shredded carrots
- » ½ cup mushrooms, thinly sliced
- » ½ cup zucchini, thinly sliced
- » ½ cup red bell pepper, finely chopped
- » ¼ cup red onion, finely chopped
- » ½ teaspoon garlic salt
- » ½ teaspoon pepper
- » 1 (13.8 ounce) tube refrigerated pizza crust dough (I used artisan-style)
- » Fresh basil, to taste
- » Marinara sauce, for dipping
- » 4 ounces mozzarella cheese, thinly sliced

Strawberry Turkey Panini

Ingredients
» Butter, as needed
» 2 Italian bread slices
» 1 tablespoon red pepper jelly
» 2 slices deli smoked turkey breast
» 1 slice Brie cheese
» 2 medium strawberries, sliced
» 1 teaspoon fresh basil, chopped

Serves 1

1. Butter one side of each slice of bread.

2. Spread the jelly on the unbuttered side of the bread.

3. Layer the remaining ingredients between slices, toast until melty, and enjoy!

Luau Melt

Serves 1

Ingredients

» Butter, as needed
» 2 Texas toast slices
» 2 tablespoons pizza sauce
» 2 slices deli ham
» 2 pineapple rings
» ⅓ cup shredded mozzarella cheese
» 5 pickled jalapeño slices

1. Butter one side of each slice of bread.

2. Spread the pizza sauce on the unbuttered side of the bread.

3. Layer remaining ingredients between slices and cook to crispy perfection. Enjoy!

Chipotle-Lime Roast Beef Sandwich

Serves 1

Ingredients

- » Butter, as needed
- » 1 pretzel roll, split
- » 1 tablespoon mayonnaise
- » 2 teaspoons lime juice
- » 2 teaspoons chipotle chili powder
- » Salt and pepper, to taste
- » 1 slice garlic-and-herb-flavored Boursin cheese
- » 2 slices deli roast beef
- » ⅓ cup red onion, sliced
- » ⅓ cup radishes, thinly sliced
- » 1 teaspoon dried rosemary

1. Butter one side of each slice of bread.
2. Mix the mayo, lime juice, chili powder, salt, and pepper; spread the mixture on the unbuttered side of the roll.
3. Layer remaining ingredients between roll halves and toast. Enjoy!

The Hot Potato

Serves 1

Ingredients

- » Butter, as needed
- » 2 Texas toast slices
- » 1 potato, sliced
- » Salt and black pepper, to taste
- » 1 teaspoon garlic powder
- » 1 tablespoon sour cream
- » ⅓ cup shredded cheddar cheese
- » 2 slices cooked bacon, crumbled
- » 2 teaspoons fresh chives, chopped

1. Butter one side of each slice of bread.
2. Fry the potato slices; season with salt, pepper, and garlic powder.
3. Spread sour cream on the unbuttered side of the bread.
4. Layer all the ingredients between bread slices and toast. Enjoy!

Fajita Sandwich

Serves 1

Ingredients

- » Butter, as needed
- » 2 potato bread slices
- » ¼ cup red onion, sliced
- » ¼ cup bell peppers, sliced
- » ¼ cup zucchini, thinly sliced
- » 1 tablespoon fajita seasoning
- » 1 queso fresco chipotle cheese wedge
- » 1 tablespoon chimichurri sauce
- » 1 slice Pepper Jack cheese

1. Butter one side of each slice of bread.
2. Sauté the veggies; stir in the seasoning.
3. Spread the cheese wedge and chimichurri on the unbuttered side of the bread.
4. Layer all the ingredients between slices and toast. Enjoy!

Cuban Sandwich

Serves 1

Ingredients

- » Butter, as needed
- » 2 sourdough bread slices
- » 2 slices Swiss cheese
- » ½ cup shredded cooked pork roast
- » 2 Canadian bacon slices
- » 1 dill pickle, sliced
- » 1 tablespoon yellow mustard

Butter one side of each slice of bread. Layer all the ingredients between the bread and toast. Enjoy!

Buffalo Chicken Waffle

Serves 2

1. Preheat your waffle iron.

2. Stir together the chicken, wing sauce, mayo, carrot, celery, and green onion.

3. Spread the mixture on two slices of bread. Sprinkle with both kinds of cheese and top each with a second bread slice.

4. Butter the outside of each bread slice and set on the hot iron. Close the lid and cook until golden brown and crisp.

5. Serve with wing sauce if you'd like. Enjoy!

TRY THIS INSTEAD

Ranch dressing has a cooling effect on buffalo chicken. Go ahead and serve these sandwiches with a side of dressing instead of wing sauce for dipping. Or dip them in both for a blast of hot AND cool.

Ingredients

- » ½ cup shredded cooked chicken
- » 2 ½ tablespoons wing sauce, plus more for dipping
- » 1 ½ tablespoons mayonnaise
- » 1 tablespoon grated carrot
- » 2 tablespoons celery, finely chopped
- » 2 tablespoons green onion, thinly sliced
- » 2 tablespoons blue cheese crumbles
- » 2 tablespoons shredded cheddar cheese
- » 4 slices ciabatta bread, about ⅜ inch thick
- » Butter, as needed

Waffle Cheeseburgers

 **Serves 5**

Ingredients

- » 1 pound lean ground beef
- » Seasonings of your choice
- » 5 cheese slices (I used American)
- » Butter, softened
- » 5 hamburger buns

1. Preheat and lightly grease your waffle iron.

2. Shape the beef into five patties, season them as you like, and set them on the hot iron. Close the lid and cook until the patties are done the way you like them. Surprise–they'll be cooked to perfection in minutes!

3. Add a slice of cheese to each burger and remove from the iron.

4. Butter the cut side of each bun, put them on the iron, and set the lid down gently on them. Cook for a minute or so until they're toasty. Assemble the burgers and enjoy!

When your burger and bun are "waffled," it just makes everything a little extra fun.

Sauces

A good waffle is made great with a delicious sauce to accompany it. Try these sauces to step up your waffle game!

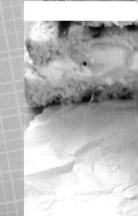

Chipotle Mayo

In a blender or food processer, blend **½ cup mayo**, **¼ cup sour cream**, **2 peppers from a can of chipotle peppers in adobo**, and the **juice of 1 lime** until finely chopped.

Creamy Honey Mustard

Store sauces in the refrigerator for up to 2 weeks.

Stir together **¼ cup mayo**, **2 tablespoons honey**, **1 tablespoon yellow mustard**, **1 tablespoon whole grain Dijon mustard**, and **2 tablespoons barbecue sauce**.

Chimichurri Sauce

In a blender or food processor, blend **½ cup each fresh parsley, fresh cilantro, olive oil, and red wine vinegar**; **¼ cup chopped onion**, **3–4 cloves minced garlic**, **1 teaspoon dried oregano**, and **½ teaspoon each salt and crushed red pepper** until finely chopped.

Sriracha Soy Ketchup

Stir together **1 cup ketchup**, **2 tablespoons brown sugar**, **2 tablespoons soy sauce**, and **1½ teaspoons sriracha**.

Dessert

◇◇◇◇◇◇◇◇◇◇◇◇◇◇◇◇◇◇◇◇◇◇◇◇◇◇◇◇◇◇◇◇◇◇◇◇

The classic waffle brings to mind sweetness, crunchiness, and blissful indulgence. These dessert waffle recipes will not disappoint. You'll get some dishes that recall those classic waffles, but also waffles that will push the boundaries and introduce you to a whole new way of waffling. All, however, are divine!

Apple Tart

 **Serves 2**

1. Coat your waffle iron lightly with oil, but don't preheat it.

2. Cut the thawed pastry to fit and set the piece(s) on the cold iron.

3. Core the apple and thinly slice it into a medium bowl. Mix the cinnamon and sugar and sprinkle about half of it over the apples; stir to coat and set the remaining cinnamon-sugar mixture aside.

4. Divide the apple slices among your pastry pieces, arranging them in a single layer; sprinkle the pecans over the apples.

5. Go ahead and close the lid right over the apples and plug in the iron. When it's a beautiful shade of golden brown and the pastry is cooked (it may need to cook several minutes after the indicator light comes on), remove the tart from the iron.

6. Sprinkle with some of the remaining cinnamon-sugar. Repeat with all the pastry pieces.

7. Warm the frosting and drizzle it over each pastry. Enjoy!

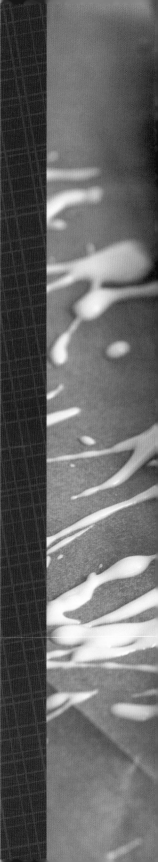

Ingredients

» 1 puff pastry sheet, thawed
» 1 baking apple (I used Gala)
» 1 ½ teaspoons ground cinnamon, divided
» 2 tablespoons sugar, divided
» 3 tablespoons pecans, chopped
» Frosting, for topping

Strawberry Shorts

Serves 6

1. Mix the berries with 3 tablespoons of the sugar and refrigerate at least 30 minutes.

2. Sift together the flour, baking powder, baking soda, salt, and 2 tablespoons sugar. Add 1 ½ cups of the whipping cream and stir until just combined. The batter will be thick!

3. Preheat and grease your waffle iron.

4. Place ¼-cup mounds of batter on the iron, close the lid, and cook until brown. Remove from the iron and set on a wire rack to cool.

5. Beat the remaining 1 ½ cups of whipping cream, remaining 3 tablespoons of sugar, and the vanilla until soft peaks form.

6. Layer the shortcakes, berries, juice, and whipping cream. Serve and enjoy!

Ingredients

» 1 ½ pounds fresh strawberries, sliced

» ½ cup sugar, divided

» 2 cups flour

» 2 teaspoons baking powder

» ¼ teaspoon baking soda

» ⅛ teaspoon salt

» 3 cups whipping cream, divided

» 1 ½ teaspoons clear vanilla

Waffle S'mores

Serves 8

Ingredients

» 2 tablespoons butter, melted
» 2 teaspoons sugar
» 2 teaspoons powdered sugar
» 1 cup milk
» 1 egg
» ⅔ cup flour
» 1 teaspoon baking powder
» ¼ teaspoon salt
» 2 tablespoons unsweetened cocoa powder
» 3 tablespoons graham cracker crumbs
» Mini marshmallows, to taste
» Mini semi-sweet chocolate chips, to taste

1. In a bowl, beat together the butter, sugar, powdered sugar, milk, and egg.

2. Sift the flour, baking powder, salt, and cocoa into the butter mixture.

3. Add the cracker crumbs and beat until well blended. The batter will be thin. Let it set 25 to 30 minutes.

4. Preheat and grease your waffle iron.

5. Pour enough batter on the iron to just cover the bottom. Close the lid and cook until just barely crisp.

6. Open the lid and put a handful of marshmallows and some chocolate chips over the front half. Carefully fold the back half over the filling and gently close the lid for a few seconds until the filling starts to melt.

7. Remove and repeat with the remaining batter. Serve and enjoy—but be careful, because that gooey filling is hot!

Dessert Chimichangas

Serves 6

Ingredients

» ¾ cup sugar

» 2 ¼ teaspoons ground cinnamon

» 1 ¾ cups ready-to-eat cheesecake filling

» 1 cup fresh strawberries and/or blueberries, coarsely chopped

» 6 (8-inch) flour tortillas

» Nonstick cooking spray

1. Combine the sugar and cinnamon on a plate or pie plate and stir until it's nicely blended; set aside.

2. Lightly grease your waffle iron and preheat it (if your iron has a browning control setting, set it on medium-high).

3. Stir together the cheesecake filling and the berries.

4. Divide the mixture evenly among the tortillas, putting the filling near the bottom of each and spreading it out slightly. Fold in the sides and roll each one up like a burrito.

5. Coat the outside of one tortilla roll with cooking spray and set it on the hot iron. Close the iron lightly and cook until it's toasty brown (you may want to flip it over at this point so the front and back become evenly browned).

6. Remove it from the iron, coat the outside again with cooking spray, and roll it in the cinnamon-sugar mixture so it's evenly coated. Now just repeat with the remaining tortillas. Serve and enjoy!

Glazed Donut Dippers

 **Serves 6**

Ingredients

- » ½ cup sugar
- » 2 teaspoons baking powder
- » ¾ teaspoon salt
- » ¼ teaspoon ground nutmeg
- » 1 egg
- » ½ cup plus 2 tablespoons milk, divided
- » 2 tablespoons butter, melted
- » 1 ½ cups flour
- » ¾ cup powdered sugar
- » 1 teaspoon vanilla, almond, lemon, or orange flavoring
- » Sprinkles, for decorating
- » Milk, for dipping

1. Stir together the sugar, baking powder, salt, and nutmeg. Add the egg, ½ cup milk, and butter; beat well.

2. Stir in the flour, mixing until thoroughly combined. The batter will be thick.

3. Preheat and grease your waffle iron.

4. Scoop the batter onto the hot iron, close the lid, and cook until golden brown.

5. Remove the waffle from the iron and set it on a wire rack to cool. Repeat with the remaining batter.

6. Stir together the powdered sugar, remaining 2 tablespoons milk, and flavoring until smooth.

7. Dip the donuts into the glaze. Return them to the rack and toss on some decorating sprinkles. Serve with a glass of milk and enjoy!!

Ice Cream Waffle Sandwiches

Ingredients
- » 1 cup sugar
- » ½ cup butter, softened
- » 2 eggs
- » ½ cup half-and-half
- » 1 ¾ cups flour
- » 1 teaspoon baking powder
- » ½ cup unsweetened cocoa powder
- » ½ teaspoon salt
- » 1 teaspoon vanilla
- » Ice cream (I used mint chocolate chip), as needed

1. Mix the sugar and butter until creamy. Add the eggs, beating until well blended.

2. Add the half-and-half, flour, baking powder, cocoa, salt, and vanilla; mix well.

3. Preheat and grease your waffle iron.

4. Drop tablespoons of dough on the hot iron, close the lid, and cook until the steaming stops. Remove them to a wire rack and repeat with the remaining dough.

5. When they're cool, fill them with ice cream and serve immediately. Or wrap individually in plastic wrap and store in the freezer for later. Enjoy!

Lemon Cake Stackers

 **Serves 14**

Ingredients

- » 1 (15.25 ounce) package lemon cake mix
- » Water, oil, and eggs as directed on cake mix package
- » 1 tablespoon lemon flavoring, divided
- » 2 cups whipping cream
- » 2 tablespoons sugar
- » Zest of 1 lemon

1. Stir together the cake mix, water, oil, and eggs as directed on cake mix package, adding 1 teaspoon lemon flavoring.

2. Preheat and grease your waffle iron.

3. Pour the batter on the iron, close the lid, and cook until light golden brown.

4. Set on a wire rack to cool. Repeat with the remaining batter.

5. Beat together the whipping cream, sugar, lemon zest, and remaining 2 teaspoons flavoring on high speed until soft peaks form.

6. Serve the cake with whipped cream. Enjoy!

Mix and match other cakes and flavorings to suit your mood and make your taste buds happy!

Apple Pie Sandwich

Ingredients

» Butter, as needed
» 2 cinnamon raisin bread slices
» 2 tablespoons mascarpone
» ¼ teaspoon honey
» 1 green apple, crisped, cored, and thinly sliced
» 2 teaspoons brown sugar
» Vanilla ice cream, for serving

Serves 1

1. Butter one side of each slice of bread.

2. Combine the mascarpone and honey and spread the mixture on the unbuttered side of the bread; add the apples and a little brown sugar.

3. Sprinkle the outside of the sandwich with more brown sugar and toast. Top with vanilla ice cream and enjoy!

Strawberry Cheesecake Sandwich

Ingredients

» Butter, as needed
» 2 slices white bread
» 2 tablespoons cream cheese, softened
» 2 tablespoons strawberry jam
» 2 strawberries, sliced
» ¼ teaspoon honey
» Fresh mint, for garnish

Serves 1

1. Butter one side of each slice of bread.

2. Spread the cream cheese and jam on the unbuttered side of the bread.

3. Layer all remaining ingredients between bread slices and toast both sides in a panini press. Enjoy!

Sweet Banana Bread Sandwich

Ingredients

» Butter, as needed
» 2 prepared slices of banana bread
» 2 tablespoons cream cheese, softened
» 2 tablespoons creamy peanut butter
» 1 tablespoon chocolate-hazelnut spread
» 1 banana, sliced
» ⅔ cup mini marshmallows

Serves 1

1. Butter one side of each slice of bread.

2. Spread the cream cheese, peanut butter, and chocolate-hazelnut spread on the unbuttered side of the bread.

3. Layer remaining ingredients between slices and toast until melty. Enjoy!

Toasted Pound Cake

Ingredients

» Butter, as needed
» 2 prepared pound cake slices
» 1 dark chocolate bar
» 1 slice Brie cheese
» 5 raspberries

Serves 1

Butter one side of each slice of bread. Layer remaining ingredients between cake slices and toast. Enjoy!

Carrot Cake

 **Serves 6**

1. Beat together the sugar, oil, and eggs.

2. In a separate bowl, stir together the dry ingredients; add them to the egg mixture and stir in the carrots until well blended.

3. Preheat and grease your waffle iron.

4. Pour the batter onto the iron, close the lid, and cook until golden brown. Remove and set on a wire rack to cool.

5. Stir the pecans into the frosting and spread over your cooled cakes. Serve and enjoy!

Ingredients

- » 2 cups sugar
- » 1 cup vegetable oil
- » 4 eggs
- » 2 cups flour
- » ½ teaspoon salt
- » 1 teaspoon baking soda
- » 1 teaspoon baking powder
- » 1 teaspoon ground cinnamon
- » 2 cups grated carrots
- » Chopped pecans, to taste
- » Cream cheese frosting, for topping

Caramel Apple Delight

Ingredients

» 2 slices angel food cake

» ½ apple, sliced

» 1 tablespoon caramel dip

» 1 tablespoon peanuts, chopped

» Cinnamon, to taste

» Sugar, to taste

Serves 1

1. Set one cake slice in a generously greased iron.

2. Cover the cake with thinly sliced apples, caramel dip, peanuts, and a generous dose of cinnamon and sugar. Add another cake slice on top.

3. Close the iron; toast until the cake has browned. Serve warm and enjoy!

Index

A

ale, in Wheat Ale Waffles, 18
apples
    Apple Gruyère Sandwich, 52
    Apple Pie Sandwich, 120
    Apple Tart, 106–7
    Caramel Apple Delight, 125
    Cinnamon-Apple Waffles, 19
artichoke sandwich with spinach, 50
avocado
    Bacon & Avocado Bites, 35
    sandwiches with, 46, 52, 54, 59, 83

B

bacon
    Bacon & Avocado Bites, 35
    Golden Waffle Frittata, 20
    other recipes with, 21, 29, 30, 46, 58,
    70–71, 79, 83, 96
    Pear and Bacon Sandwich, 55
    Toasted BLT, 43
bagels and bagel thins
    The Lox Bagel, 31
    Monte Cristo, 72
    Toasted Bagel Sandwich, 29
bananas
    Banana Bites, 24–25
    Sweet Banana Bread Sandwich, 122
Barbecue Chicken Melt, 75
Barbecue Chicken Sandwich, 42
beans, in Nacho Grilled Cheese, 52
beef
    Chipotle-Lime Roast Beef Sandwich,
    96
    Dill Corned Beef Sandwich, 91
    French Onion Steak Sandwich, 83
    Reuben Waffles, 38
    Roast Beef Sandwich, 75
    Waffle Cheeseburgers, 100–101
    Waffle-Style Corn Dogs, 62–63
Beer-Battered Shrimp, 56–57
berries
    Dessert Chimichangas, 112–13
    Strawberry Cheesecake Sandwich,
    121
    Strawberry Shorts, 108–9
    Strawberry Turkey Panini, 94
    Sweet Cinnamon Sandwich, 31
    Toasted Pound Cake, 123
brat, in The Oktober-Feast, 82
breakfast, 16–31

Banana Bites, 24–25
The Breakfast Club, 28
Cinnamon Peach French Toast, 23
Cinnamon-Apple Waffles, 19
Donut Breakfast Sandwich, 30
Easy Cherry Turnovers, 22
The Farmhand, 30
French Toast of the Town, 21
Golden Waffle Frittata, 20
Mini Muffin Crisps, 22
Quick Cinnamon Rolls, 21
Sweet Cinnamon Sandwich, 31
Toasted Bagel Sandwich, 29
Waffle-ly Good French Toast, 26–27
Wheat Ale Waffles, 18
Broccoli Cheddar Sandwich, 55
Brussels Sprout Melt, 58
Buffalo Chicken Waffle, 98–99
The Buffalo Ranch, 87

C

calzones, 48, 92–93
Canadian bacon, 29, 51, 70–71, 97
caprese sandwich, toasted, 78
Caramel Apple Delight, 125
Carrot Cake, 124
cheese. *See also* sandwiches, wraps, and
    melts
    Cheese & Onion Puffs, 44
    Cheese-Studded Waffles, 60–61
    Dessert Chimichangas, 112–13
    Eggplant Parm, 80–81
    eggs with. *See* eggs
    Hawaiian Waffle Quesadillas, 70–71
    Inside-Out Jalapeño Poppers, 45
    Parmesan Crisps, 53
    pasta with. *See* pasta
    Pizza Waffles, 68–69
    Strawberry Cheesecake Sandwich,
    121
cherry turnovers, easy, 22
chicken
    Barbecue Chicken Melt, 75
    Barbecue Chicken Sandwich, 42
    Buffalo Chicken Waffle, 98–99
    The Buffalo Ranch, 87
    Chicken & Steak Fries, 40
    Chicken & Waffles Sandwich, 90
    Chicken Parm Melt, 91
    Cobb Sandwich, 46
chimichangas, dessert, 112–13

Chimichurri Sauce, 103
Chipotle Mushroom Melt, 90
Chipotle-Lime Roast Beef Sandwich, 96
chocolate
    Ice Cream Waffle Sandwiches, 116–17
    Sweet Cinnamon Sandwich, 31
    Waffle S'mores, 110–11
cinnamon
    Cinnamon Peach French Toast, 23
    Cinnamon-Apple Waffles, 19
    Dessert Chimichangas, 112–13
    Quick Cinnamon Rolls, 21
    Sweet Cinnamon Sandwich, 31
Classic Italian, 47
Classic Reuben, 86
Cobb Sandwich, 46
The Cordon Bleu, 74
corn dogs, waffle-style, 62–63
Creamy Honey Mustard, 103
Cuban Sandwich, 97

D

dessert, 104–25
    Apple Pie Sandwich, 120
    Apple Tart, 106–7
    Caramel Apple Delight, 125
    Carrot Cake, 124
    Dessert Chimichangas, 112–13
    Glazed Donut Dippers, 114–15
    Ice Cream Waffle Sandwiches, 116–17
    Lemon Cake Stackers, 118–19
    Strawberry Cheesecake Sandwich,
    121
    Strawberry Shorts, 108–9
    Sweet Banana Bread Sandwich, 122
    Toasted Pound Cake, 123
    Waffle S'mores, 110–11
Dill Corned Beef Sandwich, 91
dinner, 66–101
    Barbecue Chicken Melt, 75
    Buffalo Chicken Waffle, 98–99
    The Buffalo Ranch, 87
    Chicken & Waffles Sandwich, 90
    Chicken Parm Melt, 91
    Chipotle Mushroom Melt, 90
    Chipotle-Lime Roast Beef Sandwich,
    96
    Classic Reuben, 86
    The Cordon Bleu, 74
    Cuban Sandwich, 97
    Dill Corned Beef Sandwich, 91

Eggplant Parm, 80–81
Fajita Sandwich, 97
French Onion Steak Sandwich, 83
The Frenchman, 82
Garden Veggie Calzones, 92–93
Gouda Mushroom Melt, 79
Guacamole Galore, 83
Hawaiian Waffle Quesadillas, 70–71
The Hot Potato, 96
Lasagna Waffles, 76–77
Leftover Spaghetti Melt, 74
Luau Melt, 95
Mac and Cheese Sammy, 87
Monte Cristo, 72–73
The Oktober-Feast, 82
Pizza Waffles, 68–69
Roast Beef Sandwich, 75
Sassy Shrimp Sammy, 78
Strawberry Turkey Panini, 94
Stromboli Sandwich, 86
Thanksgiving Leftovers, 88–89
Toasted Caprese Sandwich, 78
Toasted Turkey Sandwich, 79
Waffle Cheeseburgers, 100–101
Waffled Crabby Patties, 84–85
Donut Breakfast Sandwich, 30
donut dippers, glazed, 114–15

E

Easy Cherry Turnovers, 22
Eggplant Parm, 80–81
eggs
    Cinnamon Peach French Toast, 23
    French Toast of the Town, 21
    Golden Waffle Frittata, 20
    Toasted Bagel Sandwich, 29
    Waffle-ly Good French Toast, 26–27

F

Fajita Sandwich, 97
Faux Fry Hodge Podge, 64–65
Field of Greens Sandwich, 54
fish and seafood
    Beer-Battered Shrimp, 56–57
    The Lox Bagel, 31
    Sassy Shrimp Sammy, 78
    Stuffed Portobello Bake, 49
    Waffled Crabby Patties, 84–85
Five-Cheese Melt, 59
French Onion Steak Sandwich, 83
French toast waffles, 21, 23, 26–27
The Frenchman, 82
Fresh From the Garden Sandwich, 51

G

Garden Veggie Calzones, 92–93
Glazed Donut Dippers, 114–15
Golden Waffle Frittata, 20
Gouda Mushroom Melt, 79
greasing waffle iron, 12–13
Greek sandwich, ultimate, 46
Greek Sliders, 41
Grilled Cheese Waffles, 39
Guacamole Galore, 83

H

ham and prosciutto
    The Breakfast Club, 28
    Classic Italian, 47
    The Cordon Bleu, 74
    The Frenchman, 82
    Luau Melt, 95
    Monte Cristo, 72–73
    Prosciutto and Brie Sandwich, 54
    Stromboli Sandwich, 86
Hawaiian Waffle Quesadillas, 70–71.
    See also Luau Melt
honey mustard, creamy, 103
hot dogs, Waffle-Style Corn Dogs,
    62–63
The Hot Potato, 96

I

Ice Cream Waffle Sandwiches, 116–17
Inside-Out Jalapeño Poppers, 45
Italian, classic, 47

J

jalapeños. See peppers

K

ketchup, sriracha soy, 103

L

Lasagna Waffles, 76–77
Leftover Spaghetti Melt, 74
leftovers, Thanksgiving, 88–89
Lemon Cake Stackers, 118–19
The Lox Bagel, 31
Luau Melt, 95
lunch and snacks, 32–65
    Apple Gruyère Sandwich, 52
    Bacon & Avocado Bites, 35
    Barbecue Chicken Sandwich, 42
    Beer-Battered Shrimp, 56–57
    Broccoli Cheddar Sandwich, 55
    Brussels Sprout Melt, 58
    Cheese & Onion Puffs, 44

Cheese-Studded Waffles, 60–61
Cheesy Spinach Calzone, 48
Chicken & Steak Fries, 40
Classic Italian, 47
Cobb Sandwich, 46
Faux Fry Hodge Podge, 64–65
Field of Greens Sandwich, 54
Five-Cheese Melt, 59
Fresh From the Garden Sandwich, 51
Greek Sliders, 41
Grilled Cheese Waffles, 39
Inside-Out Jalapeño Poppers, 45
Nacho Grilled Cheese, 52
Parmesan Crisps, 53
The Peachy Keen Sandwich, 51
Pear and Bacon Sandwich, 55
Pesto Panini, 50
Prosciutto and Brie Sandwich, 54
Reuben Waffles, 38
The Sizzling Jalapeño Crunch, 58
Spicy Sausage Sandwich, 47
Spinach Artichoke Sandwich, 50
Spinach Wontons, 34
Stuffed Portobello Bake, 49
Tater Tot Flats, 36–37
Toasted BLT, 43
Turkey Pesto Sandwich, 59
Ultimate Greek Sandwich, 46
Waffle-Style Corn Dogs, 62–63

M

Mac and Cheese Sammy, 87
marshmallows
    Sweet Banana Bread Sandwich, 122
    Waffle S'mores, 110–11
mayo, chipotle, 103
Monte Cristo, 72–73
muffin crisps, mini, 22
mushrooms
    Chipotle Mushroom Melt, 90
    Faux Fry Hodge Podge, 64–65
    Garden Veggie Calzones, 92–93
    Gouda Mushroom Melt, 79
    Stuffed Portobello Bake, 49
mustard, creamy honey, 103

N

Nacho Grilled Cheese, 52

O

The Oktober-Feast, 82
onion
    Cheese & Onion Puffs, 44
    French Onion Steak Sandwich, 83

P

Parmesan Crisps, 53
pasta
    Lasagna Waffles, 76–77
    Leftover Spaghetti Melt, 74
    Mac and Cheese Sammy, 87
peaches
    Cinnamon Peach French Toast, 23
    The Peachy Keen Sandwich, 51
Pear and Bacon Sandwich, 55
peppers
    Chipotle Mayo, 103
    Chipotle Mushroom Melt, 90
    Chipotle-Lime Roast Beef Sandwich, 96
    Inside-Out Jalapeño Poppers, 45
    The Sizzling Jalapeño Crunch, 58
pesto
    Pesto Panini, 50
    Turkey Pesto Sandwich, 59
pineapple, Hawaiian dishes with, 70–71, 95
Pizza Waffles, 68–69
pork roast, in Cuban Sandwich, 97
potatoes
    Cheese-Studded Waffles, 60–61
    Chicken & Steak Fries, 40
    The Hot Potato, 96
    other recipes with, 21
    Tater Tot Flats, 36–37
pound cake, toasted, 123
puffs, cheese and onion, 44

Q

Quick Cinnamon Rolls, 21

R

Reuben Waffles and Classic Reuben, 38
Reubens, 86
Roast Beef Sandwich, 75

S

sandwiches, wraps, and melts. *See also* dessert
    Barbecue Chicken Melt, 75
    Barbecue Chicken Sandwich, 42
    The Breakfast Club, 28
    Broccoli Cheddar Sandwich, 55
    Brussels Sprout Melt, 58
    Buffalo Chicken Waffle, 98–99
    The Buffalo Ranch, 87
    Cheesy Spinach Calzone, 48
    Chicken & Waffles Sandwich, 90
    Chicken Parm Melt, 91

Chipotle Mushroom Melt, 90
Chipotle-Lime Roast Beef Sandwich, 96
Classic Italian, 47
Classic Reuben, 86
Cobb Sandwich, 46
The Cordon Bleu, 74
Cuban Sandwich, 97
Dill Corned Beef Sandwich, 91
Donut Breakfast Sandwich, 30
Fajita Sandwich, 97
The Farmhand, 30
Field of Greens Sandwich, 54
Five-Cheese Melt, 59
French Onion Steak Sandwich, 83
The Frenchman, 82
Fresh From the Garden Sandwich, 51
Garden Veggie Calzones, 92–93
Gouda Mushroom Melt, 79
Greek Sliders, 41
Grilled Cheese Waffles, 39
Guacamole Galore, 83
Hawaiian Waffle Quesadillas, 70–71
The Hot Potato, 96
Leftover Spaghetti Melt, 74
Luau Melt, 95
Mac and Cheese Sammy, 87
Monte Cristo, 72–73
Nacho Grilled Cheese, 52
Pear and Bacon Sandwich, 55
Pesto Panini, 50
Prosciutto and Brie Sandwich, 54
Roast Beef Sandwich, 75
Sassy Shrimp Sammy, 78
The Sizzling Jalapeño Crunch, 58
Spicy Sausage Sandwich, 47
Strawberry Turkey Panini, 94
Stromboli Sandwich, 86
Sweet Cinnamon Sandwich, 31
Toasted Bagel Sandwich, 29
Toasted BLT, 43
Toasted Caprese Sandwich, 78
Turkey Pesto Sandwich, 59
Waffle Cheeseburgers, 100–101
Sassy Shrimp Sammy, 78
sauces, 102–3
sauerkraut, 38, 86
sausage, 47, 76–77, 82
seafood. *See* fish and seafood
The Sizzling Jalapeño Crunch, 58
s'mores, waffle, 110–11
snacks. See lunch and snacks
spaghetti melt, leftover, 74
Spicy Sausage Sandwich, 47

spinach
    Cheesy Spinach Calzone, 48
    Lasagna Waffles, 76–77
    Spinach Artichoke Sandwich, 50
    Spinach Wontons, 34
Sriracha Soy Ketchup, 103
strawberries. *See* berries
sweets. *See* dessert

T

Tater Tot Flats, 36–37
Thanksgiving Leftovers, 88–89
Toasted Bagel Sandwich, 29
Toasted BLT, 43
Toasted Caprese Sandwich, 78
Toasted Pound Cake, 123
Toasted Turkey Sandwich, 79
tomatoes, sandwiches with. *See* sandwiches, wraps, and melts
turkey
    The Breakfast Club, 28
    Greek Sliders, 41
    Monte Cristo, 72–73
    Strawberry Turkey Panini, 94
    Thanksgiving Leftovers, 88–89
    Toasted Turkey Sandwich, 79
    Turkey Pesto Sandwich, 59
    Ultimate Greek Sandwich, 46

V

vegetables
    Faux Fry Hodge Podge, 64–65
    Fresh From the Garden Sandwich, 51
    Garden Veggie Calzones, 92–93

W

Waffle Cheeseburgers, 100–101
waffle iron
    buying, 11
    cleaning, 14–15
    greasing, 12–13
    using, 11–13, 15
waffles
    about: this book and, 9
    defined, 10
    history and evolution of, 9
Wheat Ale Waffles, 18
wontons, spinach, 34